françois cherrier

a treasure trove
of ideas

photographs by the author

translated by ruby mcmillan

angus & robertson

contents

Text of this edition © copyright
Angus and Robertson (UK) Ltd, 1973

ISBN 0 207 95536 0

Printed in Great Britain
by Colour Reproductions, Billericay

A few words about these treasures . . .

Treasure isn't always lying at the bottom of the sea! Those which this book will reveal to you are hiding . . . under your eyes. What a paradox that, every day, without a second thought, you throw them out like ordinary rubbish!

And what a pity! . . . A little imagination, and time, are all you need to create these treasures from various packaging materials (cardboard, paper, polystyrene) destined for destruction as soon as empty. Cutting up, glueing, painting can transform them into extremely decorative objects. Egg-boxes become masks or garlands of flowers; cardboard tubes, a writing-table that can be taken to pieces; large container-drums, warriors' helmets. It's an adventure, with every chance of bringing you lots of fun.

This pottering-about will bring other pleasures and benefits, too: the hands become more supple, the mind finds ingenious solutions, the whole personality expands. You'll have, as well, the satisfaction of knowing you're reversing the current trend of wasteful 'disposability'. Isn't it exciting to give new life to materials which are sacrificed to this fashion? Their cost will be light on your budget; and their origins, quickly masked and as quickly forgotten, won't prevent their astonishing you.

This book will guide you in your creations, and will, above all, inspire you to invent many others. That's the main thing: you'll learn how to look at things with new eyes, exercise your imagination, and develop that flair in seeking out 'lost' materials which will help you to complete your creations—or send you off on the scent of new ideas.

Good hunting! And don't forget that treasure reveals itself to those who have the patience to bring it to light—into full daylight.

EQUIPMENT

1 pair small scissors with pointed ends ● 1 pair household scissors ● 1 cutting-knife or scalpel (from office or artists' suppliers) ● 1 fine-toothed handsaw or picture-framer's saw ● 1 electric battery of 4·5 volts and a spool of fine wire for cutting combustible materials (artists' suppliers) ● 1 black pencil ● 1 compass ● 1 flat ruler, preferably metal ● 1 wood rasp ● 1 pair all-purpose pliers ● 1 pocket-size stapler ● 1 spool of Scotch tape ● 2 fine paint-brushes ● 1 small decorator's paint-brush, $1\frac{5}{8}$ in./4 cm. wide, rounded or fish-tailed ● 2 tubes of glue (UHU type) ● 1 box gouache ● 3 or 4 pots powdered gouache (these come in beautiful colours and are cheap) or liquid gouache (artists' suppliers) ● 3 or 4 pots matt acrylic paint ● 1 or 2 pots of lacquer paint containing glycerine ● 1-pint paint spray.

Of all the colouring materials, acrylic paint is the most versatile; it dries in 20 minutes, it is indelible; covers every surface, can be diluted in water, and every tint mixes well. But be careful to clean all brushes and stained clothing in water before the paint dries. It is an ideal medium for painting anything from a table to a puppet theatre.

MATERIALS
Aluminium foil

Also called 'silver paper', it's what covers chocolate bars. It is sold in rolls for covering food to be placed in oven or refrigerator. It exists in two thicknesses: the thicker will give you better results when making the models shown in this book. For glueing it on to paper or cardboard, use a rubber-type adhesive. On polystyrene use only a vinyl glue or a special polystyrene glue (see p. 10). Aluminium foil can be painted with a paint spray or by using acrylic paints.

Cardboard tubes and cylindrical boxes

Cardboard tubes are either used as protective packaging for materials sold rolled up; or they are the central rods on which drawing-paper, dress material, etc. are rolled. You'll find these in your home in the middle of rolls of kitchen foil or of drawing paper or as tubes for sending such things as calendars, drawings, etc. through the post. You can also find them in large numbers among the rubbish thrown out by, for instance, architects' offices: ask them to reserve these for you; they'll be happy to render you this little service.

Cylindrical boxes are used as packaging for many products you'll find at the supermarket. We have chosen three sizes of diameter: $7\frac{7}{8}$ in./20 cm., 9 in./23 cm. and 11 in/28 cm.

For cutting barrels and tubes, or to join these together, proceed as shown in figure A: with the aid of a cutting-knife with a short, well-sharpened fixed blade (see illustration opposite), cut the cardboard by directing the cutting edge of the knife away from yourself, cutting with a short backwards and forwards movement, following the traced line. Keep your left hand as far as possible away from the knife.

For the right-angled assemblage of two tubes of different diameters, first trace on the larger tube the part to be cut away, as follows: take a bit of the small tube and, with the aid of your wood rasp, make its end concave so that it can be adapted to the larger tube. On the larger tube you will then trace the hole to be cut out so that the smaller tube can be pushed into it. Make the same tracing on the opposite side of the large tube, in such a way that the smaller tube will go through in a straight line, then cut out the two holes you've traced, as indicated above.

To make perfect straight or 45° cuts in your tubes, you can use a little mitre-box (fig. B) and a picture-framer's saw: hold the tube firmly within the mitre-box, and saw. To cut a series of tubes to the same length, or to open up a slot in your tube, make a pencil mark inside the mitre-box at the place corresponding to that in the tube's length where you wish your cut or slot to be made, as a guide to your saw.

For glueing, use any good paper-and-cardboard glue (UHU particularly recommended).

Use coarse sandpaper to smooth cut edges. To rub off shaggy bits of the cardboard use a finer sandpaper.

To paint correctly and achieve a smooth finish, paint on first an undercoat of white matt acrylic paint (or, next-best, a washable paint) which will cover any printing or other marks on the cardboard and will help you to do away with any remaining nap on the cardboard (which you can sandpaper away after the undercoat has dried). You will thus obtain a more resistant surface and more vivid colour from subsequent coats of paint. Any type of paint will do for these. If you wish to obtain the best results, use a paint spray. For a quick painting job, use gouache or two coats of acrylic paint.

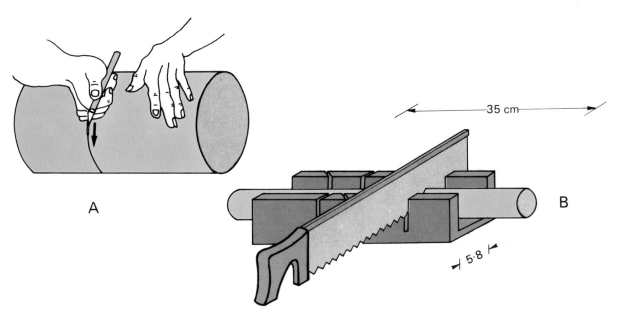

A

35 cm

5.8

B

Moulded Cardboard

The soft material used in making cardboard can be moulded before it dries. It is thus that packaging for fragile objects and certain foods is created. The two sides of moulded cardboard are always different: one is almost smooth, the reverse rough and grainy. It can be beige or grey or mauve tinted. Large platter-like containers for eggs have 30 'cups' (fig. 1) and nest into one another, or stand on top of one another when filled with eggs. They are obtainable in two different cup sizes; of course one must stick to one size for each object being made. It's very easy to obtain these from tradesmen who have no further use for them.

The most currently-used egg-boxes come in three different models; to distinguish between them we shall use the following expressions: 'egg-boxes with rounded cups' (fig. 2), 'egg-boxes with angular cups' (fig. 3), 'egg-boxes with shallow rounded cups' (fig. 4). All the boxes we shall be using have 6 cups, but you can make most of the models from larger boxes. The moulded platters with indentations for fruit are generally mauve, all the same size, but with more or fewer indentations according to the size of the fruit packaged; as with the 30-egg platters, ask tradesmen for these.

If our examples are limited to these two types of packaging, it's because they are the most widely distributed. In nearly all packaging there is something interesting to be found—see, for example, the mask of Babar the Elephant on p. 35.

For cutting out, use small scissors with pointed ends and a small knife with well-sharpened blade, or, better still, a cutting-knife with short fixed blade—very practical for cutting up many different materials. For glueing, use any paper and cardboard glue. For painting: gouache, acrylic paint or paints in sprays.

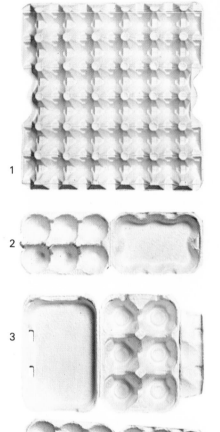

1
2
3
4

Expanded polystyrene

Usually white, this material's distinguishing characteristic is its lightness. It is made up of an infinite number of closed micro-cells, larger or smaller, coarse-grained or fine, according to the use it is intended for: as insulating panels for buildings; in slabs and blocks for sculpture, scale models, decorations, packaging, etc. The most resistant is that used for packaging. Because it is easy to work with and has a good finish polystyrene is the ideal material for a great many creations. Most of the objects made from expanded polystyrene explained in this book, have been fashioned from the covers of fish-boxes. As the packaging is impervious to water, it is easy to clean. You'll find many other packages with a smooth surface: the packaging for boxes of washing powder, for books, fruit, glass, publicity matter, etc. Because of their diversity, we've also used polystyrene egg-boxes.

For cutting out you will need:

1) A cutting-knife with a fixed blade which is short, thick and above all, well sharpened.

2) A scalpel or, better still, a cutting-knife with interchangeable blades; all this equipment on sale at office or artists' suppliers.

3) An appliance which heats wire for cutting combustible materials. There are several different models, usually sold for use in electrical pokerwork.

4) An appliance (fig. A) or a little hot-wire cutter (fig. B) which you can make yourself by buying special alloy wire, $\frac{1}{16}$th in./1·5 mm. in diameter which is used in the appliances sold commercially (the 10-yard (10 m.) spool of wire can be bought at a reasonable price.) With the little apparatus (fig. A) you can do all your cutting easily and safely: hold the electric battery, press the metal flange and direct the wire to the slab of polystyrene, keeping the wire at right angles to the polystyrene. To stop the cutting, remove the index finger from the metal flange and cutting will stop at once.

For clever handy-men we would recommend making the little hot-wire cutter (fig. B) which enables one to do varied jobs, and gives a perfect cut. It presents no danger, as the wire heats up very little and cools immediately you release the switch.

To cut at right angles to the table and in a straight line, using a T square for guidance, place your wire upright while shifting the drawing-board, then tighten the two vices: place your length of polystyrene on the board and slide it along under the wire, holding it steady while pressing on the foot-switch, and pushing down the hot wire. For a circular cut (a wheel or a cylinder) proceed as shown in sketch C: the distance from the nail to the wire is equal to the radius of the cylinder you wish to make.

To level off surfaces or edges, rub very gently with fine sandpaper. For glueing use a vinyl glue or a special polystyrene adhesive (e.g. Bostik or UHU), avoiding all others, which would corrode the polystyrene. Or a spray containing these types of adhesive would be suitable. To colour, use acrylic paint or gouache, or spray with metallic or fluorescent paint (obtainable in many colours) or varnish. Lacquer paints containing glycerine should be tried out first or separated from the polystyrene surface with an undercoat of white acrylic paint. Of course, when using a paint spray care should be taken not to ruin surrounding walls, furniture, etc.

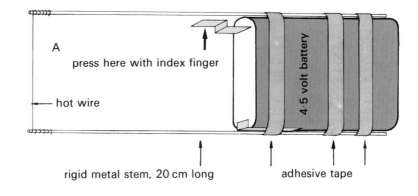

A

press here with index finger

hot wire

rigid metal stem, 20 cm long

4·5 volt battery

adhesive tape

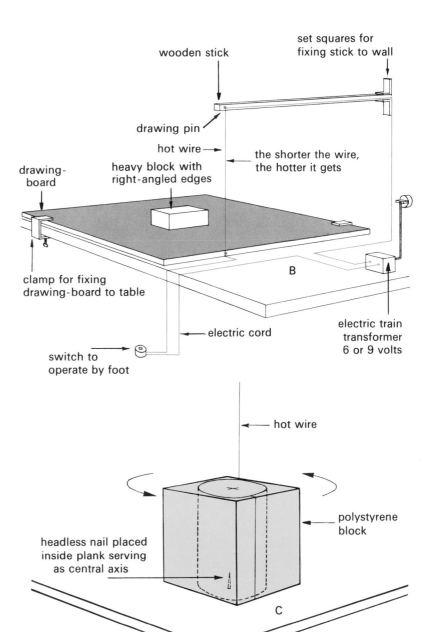

wooden stick

set squares for fixing stick to wall

drawing pin

hot wire

the shorter the wire, the hotter it gets

drawing-board

heavy block with right-angled edges

clamp for fixing drawing-board to table

B

electric cord

electric train transformer 6 or 9 volts

switch to operate by foot

hot wire

polystyrene block

headless nail placed inside plank serving as central axis

C

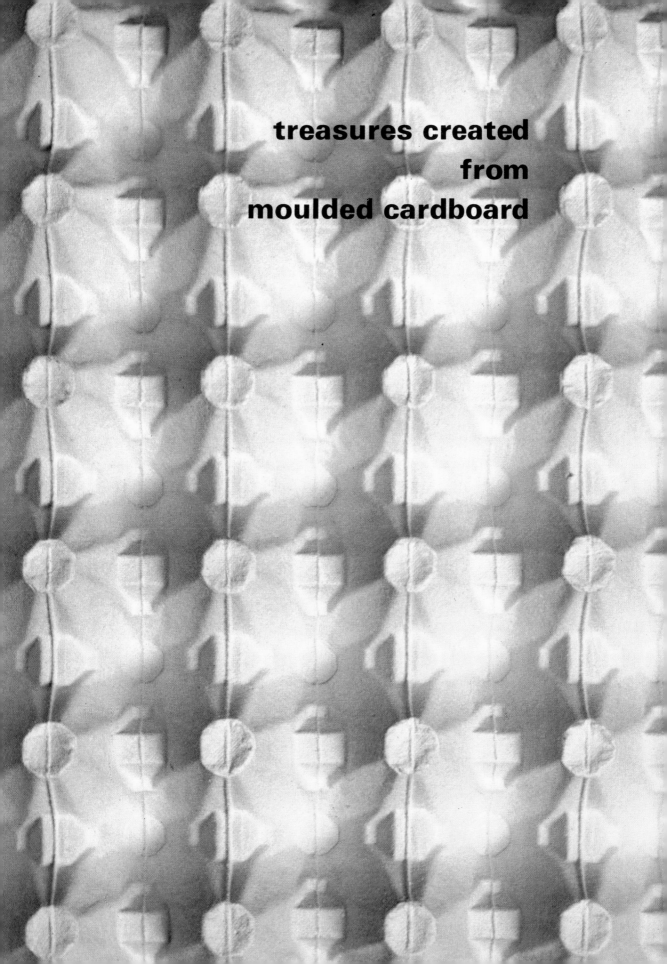

treasures created
from
moulded cardboard

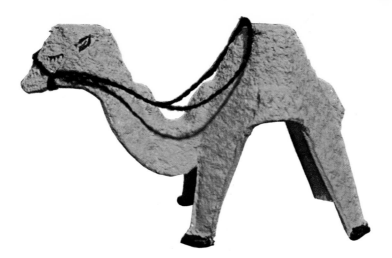

The camel

Equipment: a 30-egg container; a strand of black wool; yellow-ochre and black gouache.

In the photo below, it is the grainy-surfaced side of the egg-box that you see. The camel is seen as if from an aeroplane; the top of his hump is the top of one of the inverted 'cups' of the base of the egg-box. His head occupies a neighbouring summit; his feet are in the pits between the cup bases. Sketch the outlines in pencil on your cardboard container and cut out with small scissors. Paint the body yellow-ochre and the eyes, ears, and feet black. For the harness, pass a strand of black wool through two holes pierced, one on either side of his mouth.

The caravan

Equipment: a 30-egg container; black wool; gouache.

A single egg-box base is sufficient for making 15 camels. The saddle A and the double basket B are shown in the photo below near the dromedary. Compare the photograph with your own egg-box and, with a stroke of your pencil, mark out the corresponding areas. Cut out and paint with gouache. Glue the saddle or basket to the top of the camel's humps.

The bathyscape

Materials: 1 30-egg container; 5 opaque beads; 1 piece thin cardboard 3⅞ in./10 cm. square; gouache; glue.

Cut out 5 portions A and 5 portions B as shown in figure 1: the surface of the container which you see is the very grainy one; compare your egg-container with the one in the picture; sketch in pencil the outlines of these portions and cut out. Glue 4 portions B in the form of a cross, joining them by their points. Place these 4 joined portions over your piece of cardboard and with a pencil trace the outline of their lower opening on to the cardboard; this will be the bathyscape's floor, which should be cut out and glued to the opening. For the pilot: glue 3 opaque beads, one on top of the other, then paint his face and suit. Glue the pilot to the middle of the floor and close the cabin by glueing on the fifth portion B. Glue on the headlights: 2 portions A with a bead in each cavity. Glue on the jets portions A glued to the ends of portions B. Paint the bathyscape red.

Venetian lanterns

Materials: 1 30-egg container; red cellophane or transparent candy paper; red cotton thread; glue; black and gold or silver matt paint.

For each lantern, cut out two portions like the one shown in figure 2, from the smooth side of the container. Glue the portions together at their points. Knot the end of a length of cotton thread. Pass the thread through the interior of each lantern, letting it emerge through the hole you have pierced in the top. Paint matt black. Over each opening glue a piece of cellophane, trimming off the edges after the glue has dried. Decorate with gold or silver paint.

1

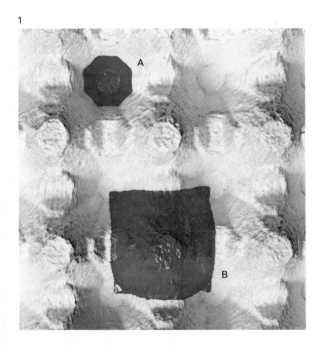

2

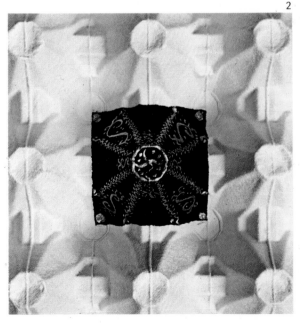

Flowers

Materials: moulded 30-egg container; egg-box with rounded cups; egg-box with angular cups (see p. 10); strong galvanized iron wire in 11¾ in./30 cm. lengths; opaque beads, ¼ in./8 mm. and ¾ in./18 cm. diameters (failing these, use pearls); matches or sticks of balsa wood all the same size; pins; glue; gouache.

In the photos below, the six principal flowers of the bouquet are shown outlined on their respective containers. The flowers in figures 1, 3 and 5 are on the moulded 30-egg platter. Those in figures 2 and 4 are on the egg-box with rounded cups; and the flower in figure 6 on a box with angular cups. Outline your flowers in pencil on their respective packets, then cut out. Push the glue-coated tip of a balsa wood stick into an opaque bead, then stick the tip of one of your galvanized-iron wire 'stems' into the free end of the balsa stick. Paint the flower and its centre. Push your wire higher until it pierces the interior of your flower, having first pierced the centre of the corolla and covered the lower surface of the bead with glue. Stick the bead at the base inside the flower and hold while the glue dries. On certain flowers make pistil and stamens by sticking into this bead pins whose heads have already been covered with a smaller glass bead or a pearl.

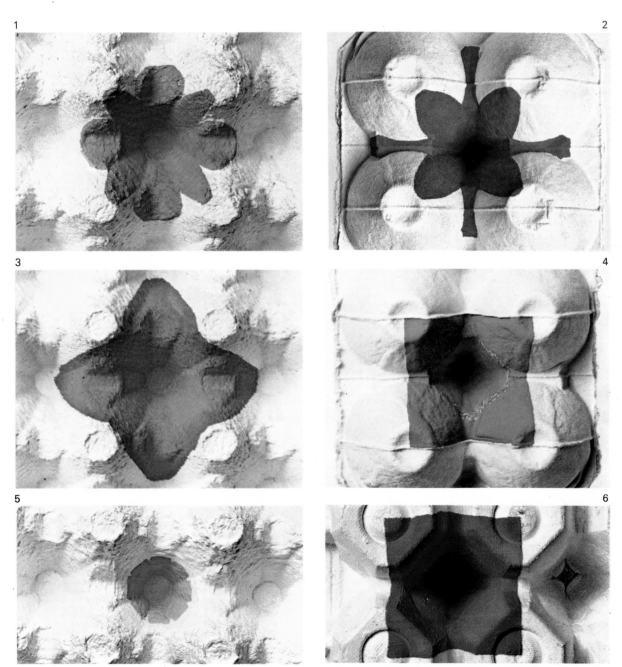

1

2

3

4

5

6

A garland of flowers

Materials: a moulded 30-egg container; gouache.

The photo on the right shows the garland painted on to the platter's smooth surface, cut on a diagonal. Cut out and paint with gouache.

A mobile

Materials: a moulded 30-egg container; piano wire (toyshops and model-making shops); 3 cellulose balls $1\frac{1}{8}$ in./3 cm. diameter (or cork balls); 7 opaque beads; a cube of balsa or expanded polystyrene, $\frac{1}{2}$ in./13 mm. each side; matches, thick cardboard; glue; gouache or acrylic paint.

Cut out 7 units like that in figure 1 (grainy side of the cardboard). Glue one unit on each surface of the cube. Cut out 3 pieces of cardboard $4\frac{3}{4}$ in./12 cm. square, out of one of which a 'window' has been cut (see sketch below). Cut 5 lengths of piano wire, measuring $15\frac{3}{4}$ in./39 cm., $11\frac{3}{8}$ in./29 cm., 11 in./28 cm., $9\frac{1}{2}$ in./24 cm. and $7\frac{7}{8}$ in./20 cm. respectively. At $1\frac{5}{8}$ in./4 cm. from their ends, bend the wires to form triangles and pass them through the top cardboard square, in which you have already cut 4 slits (see fig. 2). Fix the stems to the cardboard with adhesive tape. Glue the 3 cardboard squares together. Push the cube (which you have already pierced) firmly down on to the longest stem, to make the focus of your creation. On the $11\frac{3}{8}$ in./29 cm. stem place the final cut-out unit by piercing its centre. At the end of the stem place an opaque bead, joining them together with the help of a small glue-covered piece of matchstick. Cover the lower part of the bead with glue and hold in contact with the cut-out unit. On the other stem place the 1 in. balls, treating them in the same manner. Paint as shown in the photo opposite. Deep inside each is a gradation of red, sprayed on, or applied with a paintbrush. Paint 6 beads black and glue into the troughs of the units attached to the cube.

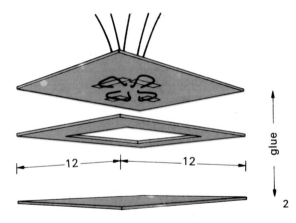

1

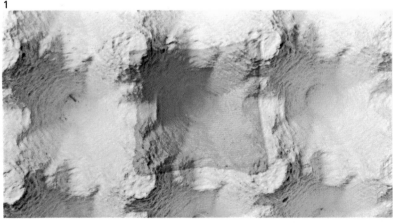

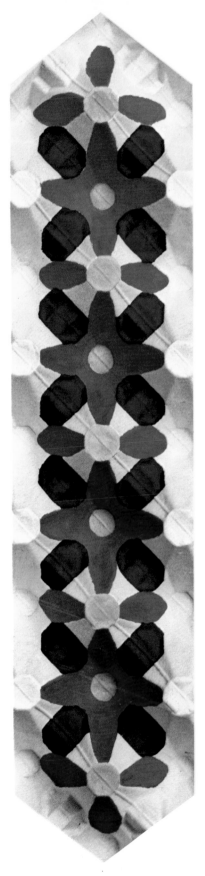

Clowns

Materials: 30-egg container; gouache

Figure 1 shows the back view of a clown, painted on the grainy side of the packaging. Sketch his position on the egg-box, by drawing his outline in pencil. The hands and feet of the clown are in the bottoms of 4 cups, and the top of one is the arch of his back. Cut out and paint as you fancy.

LITTLE GIFTS

Materials: egg-boxes with rounded cups (see p. 10); glue; gouache or acrylic paint.

An egg-cup

Cut out of the box the two parts of the packaging shown in figure 2. Glue the two tops together and decorate to your taste.

Stands for hard-boiled eggs and for salt

Figure 3 shows the hard-boiled egg stand in the packaging, with the box open. The salt cellar is made in the same way, but omit two cups. Cut out, and paint as you wish.

Dressing-table tidy

Use the cover of the box. Indent the sides as shown in the photo opposite. Even off the edges with scissors and decorate.

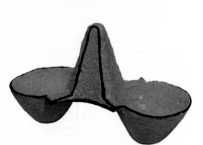

1

2

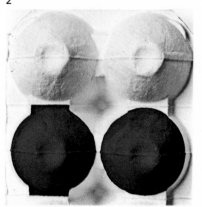

3

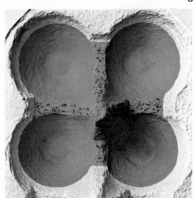

22

23

Super-spider

Materials: 30-egg container; one egg-box, rounded cups (see p. 10); an opaque glass bead, glue, gouache; a piece of cardboard $5\frac{7}{8}$ in./15 cm. square.

From the 30-egg container cut out double examples of the hat, A, and the legs, B and C (fig. 1). To facilitate your work mark their positions on the container by tracing their outlines in pencil, with the grainy side of the packet facing you. Now cut out the body of the spider from an egg-box with rounded cups (fig. 2). Glue legs and head to the inner surface of the body after marking their positions as shown in the photo above. Glue an opaque bead inside the hat, to make the head. Paint the spider lilac and speckle with yellow and orange. Glue the spider to the cardboard square.

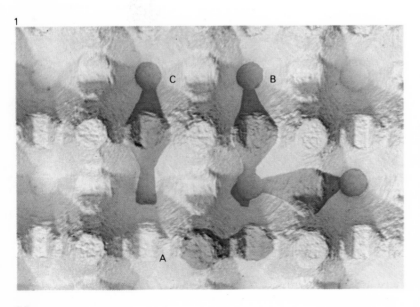

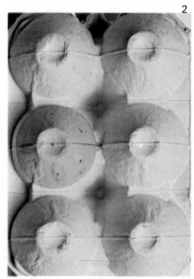

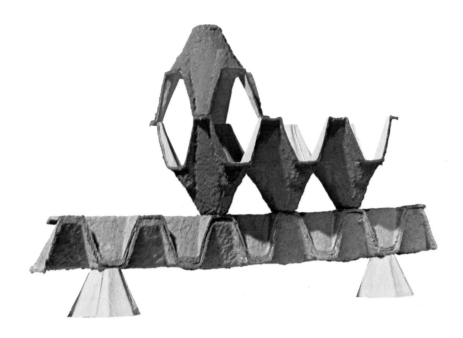

Monorail train

Materials: 30-egg container; glue; gouache.

As in the figure below, indicate the place of each unit on your container sheet, drawing the outline in pencil. Cut out all the portions, cutting D twice. At the front of the train (A), glue on the top part of the cabin (B) by its 4 points. For the rail, glue the two units D inverted, against one another. Glue the two supports (C) to the rail. Now glue the monorail train on to the rail. Paint in gouache.

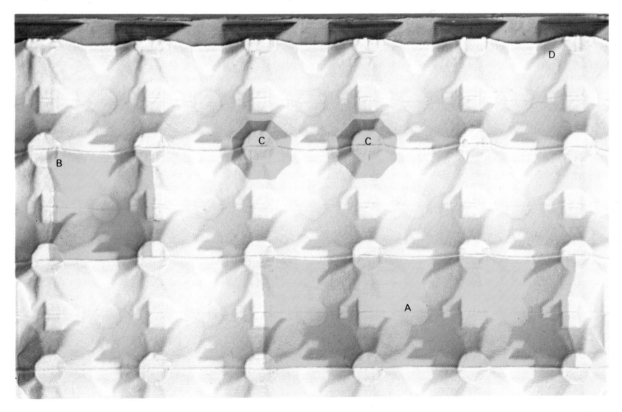

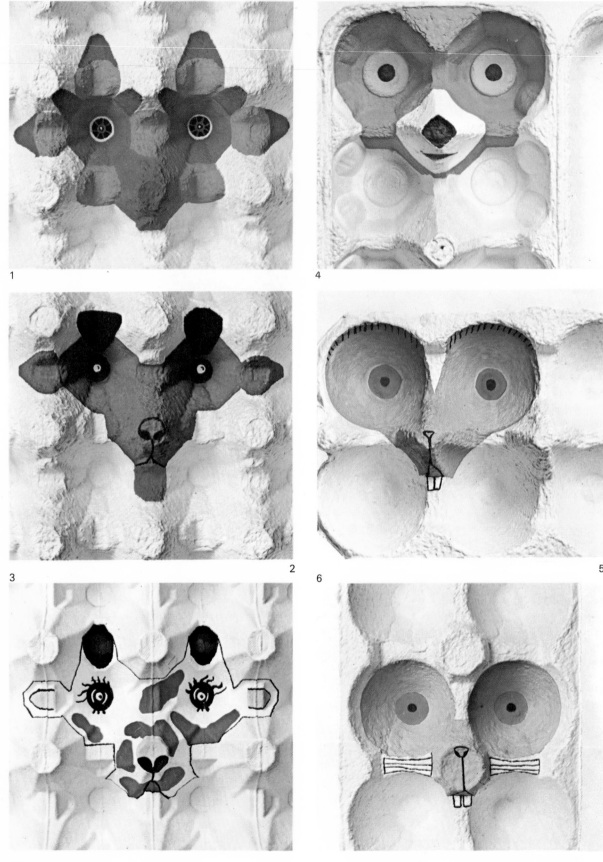

1

4

3

2

6

5

Masks (for children)

Materials: 30-egg container; egg-box with rounded cups; egg-box with angular cups; egg-box with shallow rounded cups (see p. 10); twine; elastic; gouache.

The masks are shown on their respective packagings, so as to indicate the portions to be cut out. The rat, above, is shown in figure 5. The masks in figures 1, 2, 3, 7 and 8 are cut from a 30-egg container; figure 4 from an egg-box with angular cups. The masks in figure 5 is cut from an egg-box with rounded cups, and the head in figure 6 from an egg-box with shallow rounded cups. Trace each head on its respective packet and cut out. (The head in figure 8 is at the edge of the 30-egg container.) Paint as indicated in each figure. For the rat's whiskers, pass a length of untwisted twine through two holes pierced in its muzzle. For the bear's mouth (fig. 4), slit the base of the muzzle with a cutting-knife; open the mouth gently and paint the interior pink. To make masks, pierce holes through the middle of the eyes (at the bottom of the cups), then pass two ends of pieces of elastic through the holes, and knot.

7

8

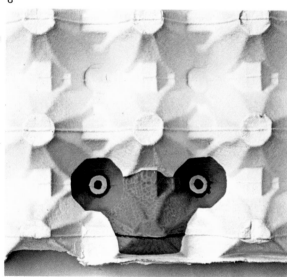

27

A prehistoric beast

Materials: a 30-egg container; glue; gouache.

As shown in figure 2, mark on your container the position of each portion, by drawing the outlines in pencil. Use the grainy surface of the packet. Cut out all the parts. Assemble and glue them together in order from A to E (see fig. 1). Paint the body green and do the eyes and spots as shown in the photo opposite.

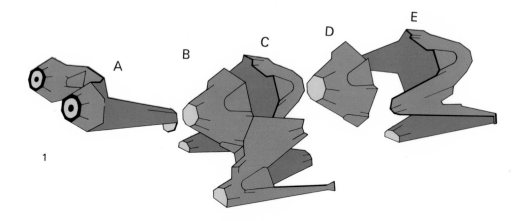

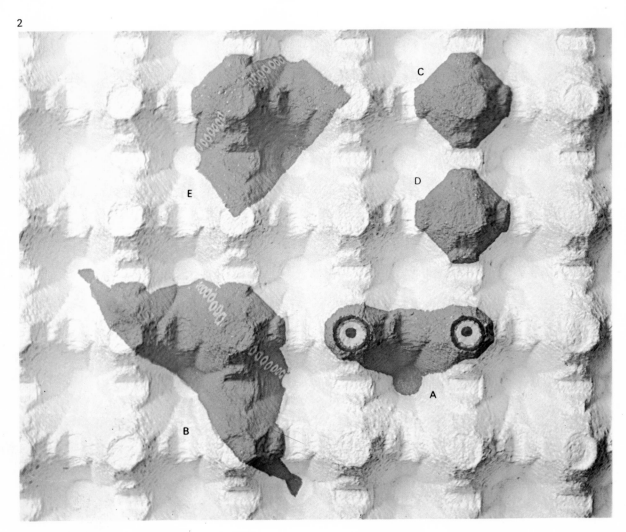

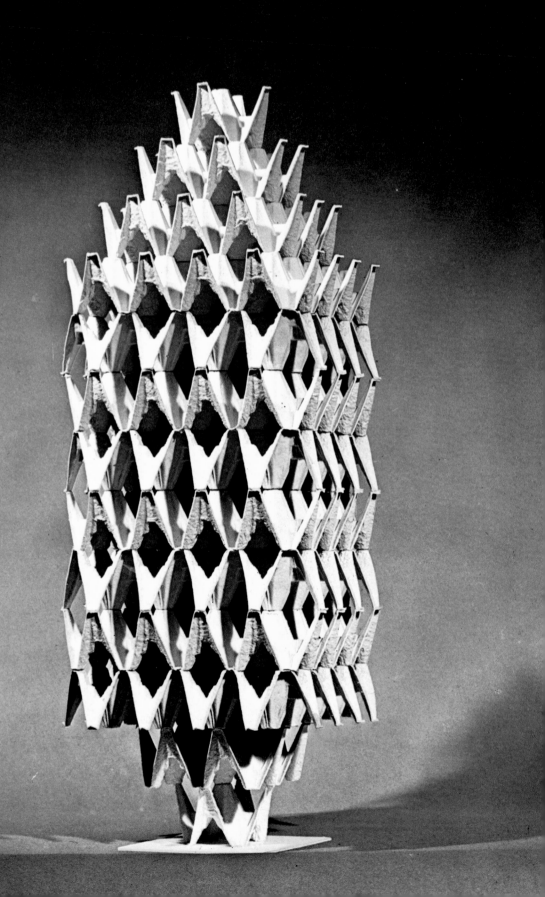

Bedside lamp

Materials: 3 moulded 30-egg containers; 4 squares of red transparent plastic $3\frac{1}{2}$ in $\times$ $3\frac{1}{2}$ in./9 cm.; strong cardboard, $\frac{1}{8}$ in./3 mm. thick; electric light bulb (40 watt), light socket, electric cord, wall plug; glue; black acrylic paint; gilt paint in a spray.

The lamp consists of 6 different levels, cut out and made up as follows: 1) the tip of an inverted cup and 4 points; 2) 4 tips and 8 points; 3) 9 tips and 12 points; 4), 5) and 6) similarly to 3), 2) and 1) respectively. The central portion of the lamp is cut out at its base to receive the bulb and light socket. Cut out the 6 levels and paint them gold. For the pedestal, cut out of cardboard, 2 squares $3\frac{3}{4}$ in./9·5 cm. $\times$ $3\frac{3}{4}$ in. 2 rectangles of $3\frac{3}{4}$ in./9·5 cm. $\times$ $1\frac{3}{8}$ in/3·5 cm.; and 2 others of $3\frac{1}{2}$ in./9 cm. $\times$ $1\frac{3}{8}$ in./3·5 cm. Glue together as though making a box, inserting the electric wire through one side of the base and upwards to meet the light socket. Glue all the levels of the lamp onto the base, one on top of another; then glue the squares of transparent plastic on each surface of the lamp between six points. Paint the base black.

The tower

Materials: 11 30-egg containers; glue, cardboard $5\frac{1}{8}$ in./13 cm. square.

The tower consists of 13 levels, as shown in the illustration opposite. They are made up, from top to bottom, as follows: 1) the tip of an inverted cup and 4 points; 2) 4 tips and 8 points; 3) 9 tips and 12 points; 4), 5), 6), 7), 8), 9), 10) and 11), 16 tips and 16 points; 12) 4 tips and 8 points; 13) 1 tip and 4 points. Cut out and glue the levels in that order. Glue on to a base of cardboard.

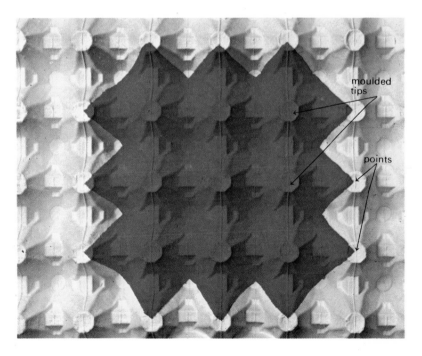

moulded tips

points

Modern Sculpture I

Materials: 30-egg containers; red and yellow transparent plastic, $2\frac{1}{2}$ in./6·5 cm. square; cork balls $1\frac{3}{4}$ in./4·5 cm. diameter; cardboard; glue; paint.

The photo opposite shows a sculpture composed of: 23 units like the one shown in fig. 1; 9 cork balls painted red; 6 plastic squares, 3 yellow and 3 red. All parts are assembled, glued together, then glued onto a cardboard base. Or, using the same pieces, create your own original sculpture.

1

Modern Sculpture II

Materials: 30-egg containers; piano wire; cellulose balls of different sizes; cardboard; glue; paint spray containing green metallic paint.

The photograph below shows a 'sculpture' composed of: 30 units like the one in fig. 2; 3 cellulose balls painted red and threaded on a piece of piano wire; a base of $3\frac{1}{8}$ in./8 cm. square cardboard. Glue all together and spray on paint. This is given as only one example of the many attractive sculptures you can assemble by this means.

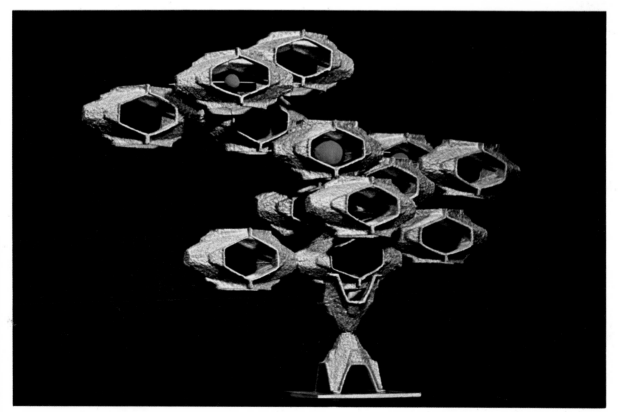

2

The little elephant

Materials: Moulded cardboard packaging for three bottles of champagne; 2 cardboard tubes $\frac{1}{2}$ in./1·5 cm. diameter and $3\frac{1}{8}$ in./8 cm. long; strong elastic; glue; grey and white acrylic paint (or gouache).

The packaging consists of two similar portions; cut away one of these as shown in the sketch. Glue the tusks (carboard tubes) on behind. Pierce two little holes for the eyes (see sketch). Paint the whole thing grey, using a lighter grey for the ears. The tusks and outlines of the eyes are in white. Behind the mask at the level of the eyes, pierce a hole in the neck of each of the bottle cases and knot the two ends of the elastic there.

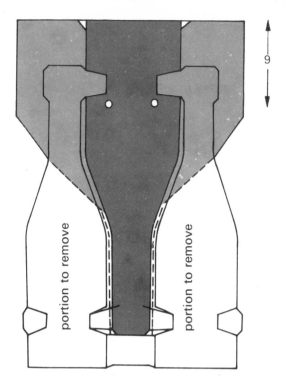

Fruit salver (a present for Mother)

Materials: a moulded cardboard platter for packaging fruit; white acrylic paint; fine sandpaper; red laquer paint.

Choose a platter in good condition. Cut the outside edge in such a manner as to slightly open out the first moulds. Paint both surfaces with an undercoat of white acrylic paint. Allow to dry for 2 hours, then rub the edges with sandpaper. Apply 3 coats of red laquer: the carton will thus become very solid and will withstand cleaning.

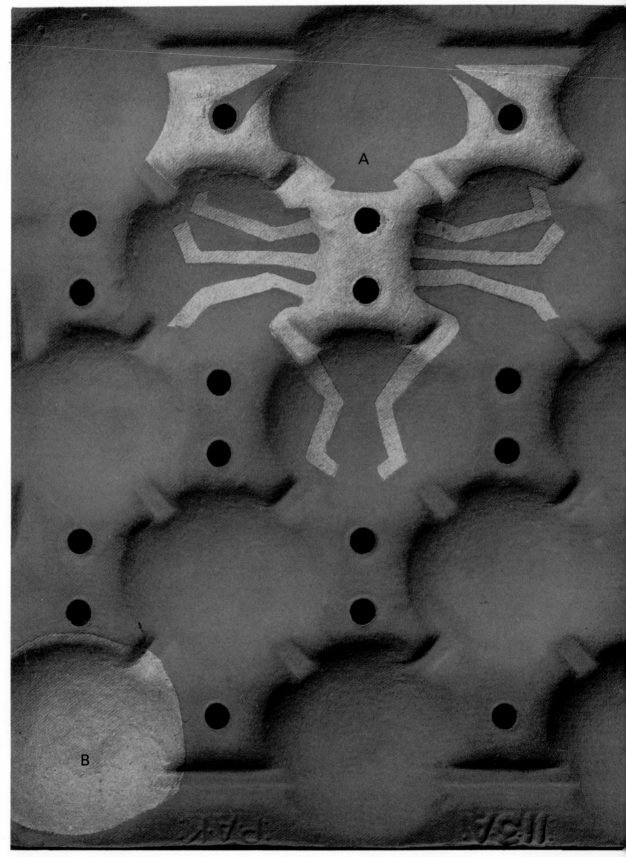

The crab

Materials: a moulded cardboard platter used in fruit packaging; 2 small opaque beads or pearls; glue.

The crab consists of three parts: A, B, B' (B' is similar to B but not shown on the figure opposite). Trace in pencil the outline of each part, on your platter. Cut out the three sections. Glue the two shells (B and B') on top of one another, superimposing the eye cavities which will receive the two little beads or pearls. Glue the body thus formed on to the flat section between the legs (A). Paint the eyes orange, the body black, brown, green, etc., as you please.

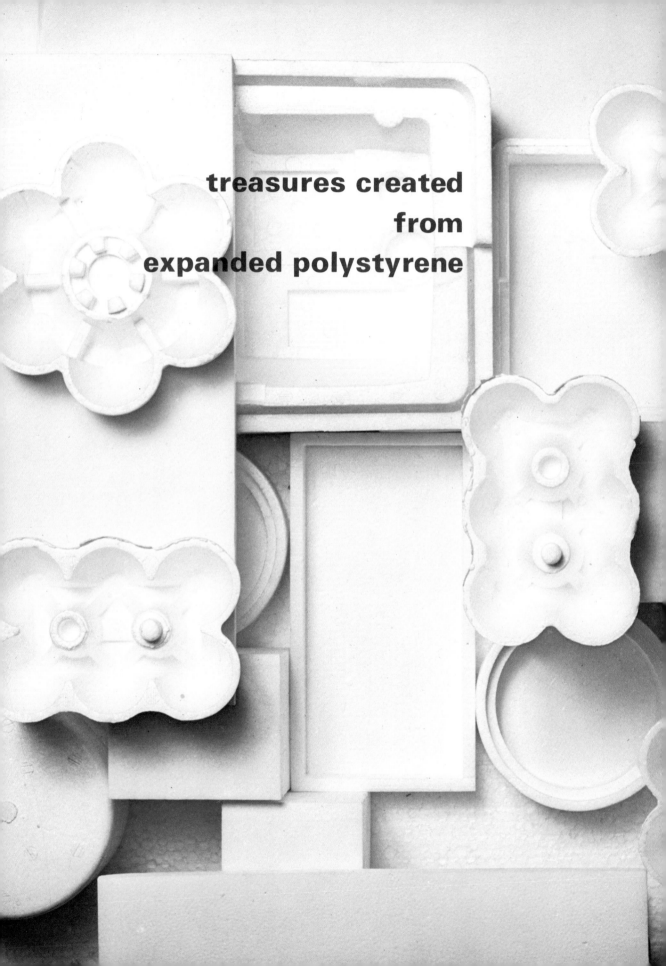

treasures created
from
expanded polystyrene

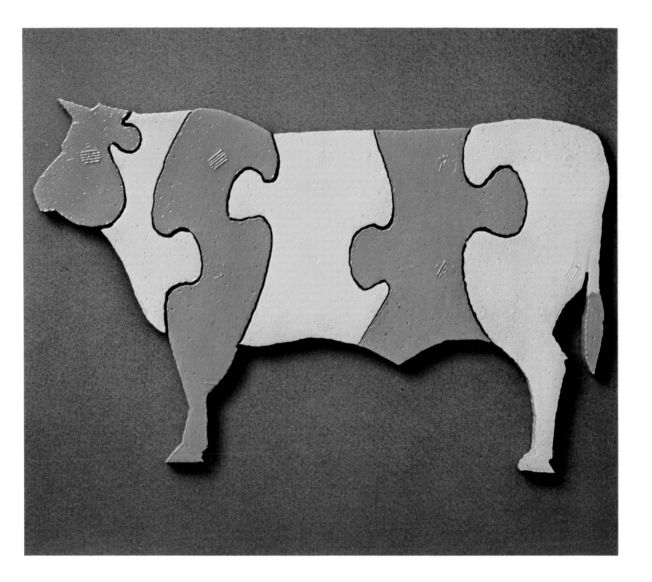

A Beef-joint puzzle

Materials: a plaque of expanded polystyrene 11 in./28 cm. square; tracing paper; fine sandpaper; acrylic paint; terra-cotta and chrome yellow.

Holding tracing-paper over the photo of the bull, above, trace his silhouette and the outlines of the 'jigsaw' cuts. On the reverse of your paper go over the lines you have traced. Place your paper, right side up, on the polystyrene and mark out the design. Cut out each piece (see p. 11). With sandpaper, rub gently round the outline of the bull's silhouette. Paint each piece as shown in the photo.

Tough dog

Materials: Expanded polystyrene lid from a fish crate measuring 15¾ in./40 cm. × 11 in./25 cm.; tracing-paper; fine sandpaper, black/laquer paint (with glycerine); 2 rounds of orange paper ⅜ in./1 cm. in diameter; 2 rounds of black paper ¼ in./6 mm. in diameter; vinyl glue.

Trace the whole design, from the double page spread on the following pages. On the reverse of your tracing, go over all your lines. Place the tracing, right side up on the polystyrene and mark out the design. Cut out (see p. 11). Rub gently with sandpaper, the surfaces and edges of each cut out section, until they are smooth. Glue the portion A' of leg 1 on to A; the portion B' of leg 2 on to B. Following the dotted lines of the design, glue legs 3 and 4 into place. Laquer the dog black. When completely dry, glue first the orange discs for his eyes, then the black discs for the pupils.

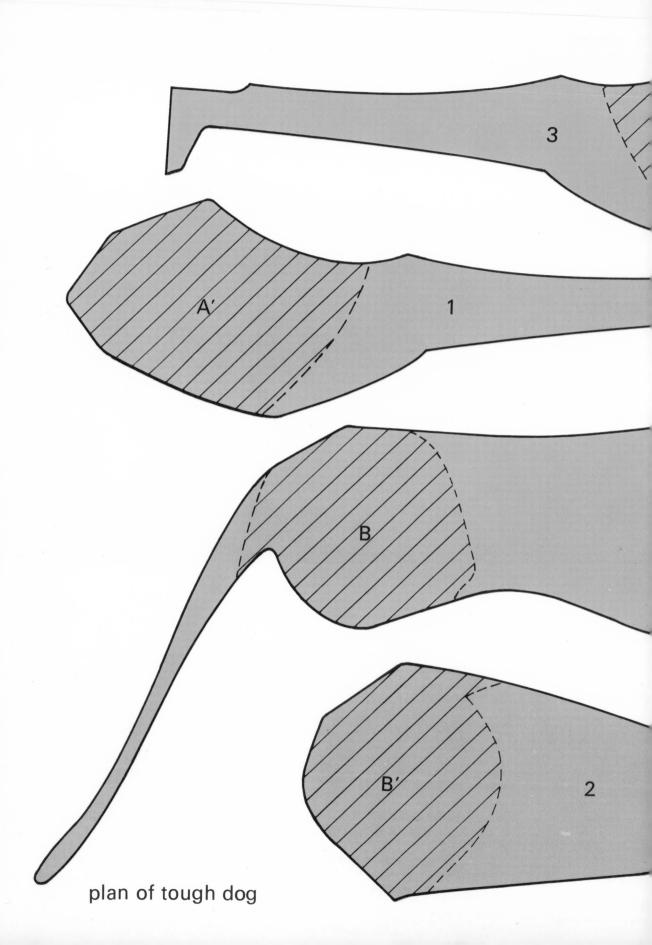

plan of tough dog

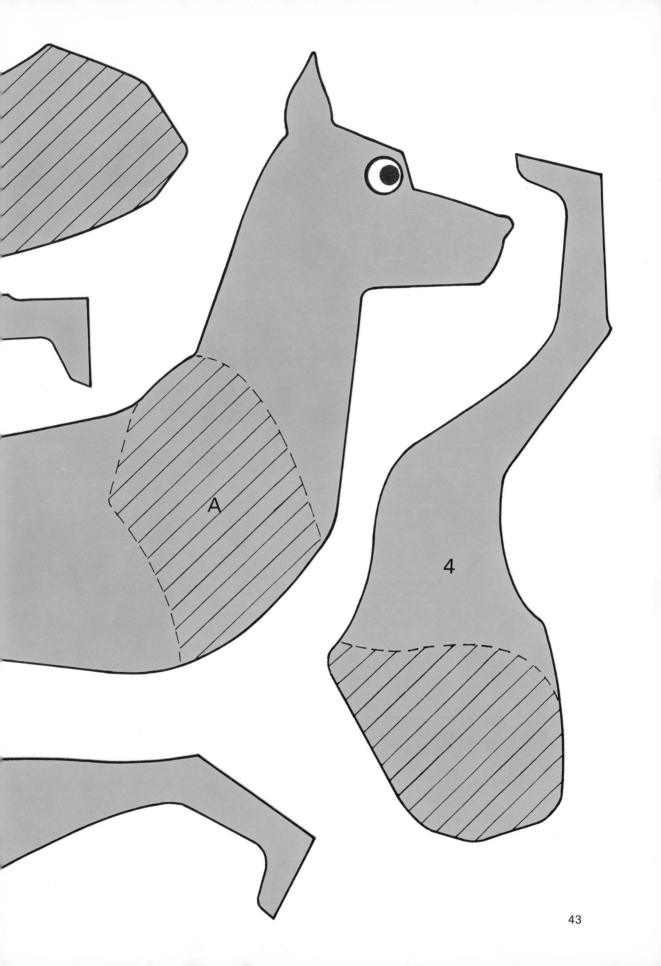

A

4

An old jaloppy

Materials: 2 polystyrene fish-crate lids, one $\frac{3}{4}$ in./17 mm. thick, the other $\frac{1}{2}$ in./12 mm. thick; vinyl glue; pins; acrylic paint.

From the $\frac{3}{4}$ in./17 mm. polystyrene cut out (see p. 11) the chassis and the bonnet to the dimensions indicated below. The bonnet is cut out of the edge of the lid, to take advantage of its rounded shape. Cut all the other parts out of the $\frac{1}{2}$ in./12 mm. thick polystyrene. The sides of the car should be cut out by reversing the pattern when cutting out the second side. For the wheels, cut four circles $1\frac{5}{8}$ in/4 cm. in diameter from the $\frac{1}{2}$ in/12 mm. thickness. To facilitate the cutting out you can draw rectangles to represent each surface of the car, as shown in the drawing. Glue the parts together and attach the wheels with pins. Paint.

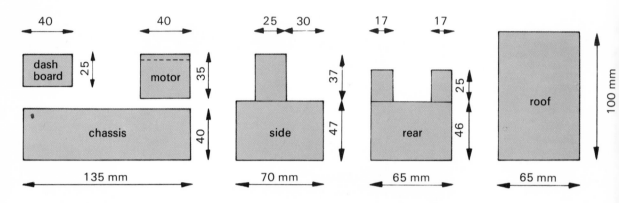

Dish for salted party-snacks

Materials: 2 round 6-egg expanded polystyrene boxes; vinyl glue; fine sandpaper; red laquer paint (containing glycerine).

From the two parts of a box, cut out in a circle the central section, following the centre of each cup. You can do this cutting with a cutting-knife with a fine and well-sharpened blade. Rub the cut surfaces gently with sandpaper. Assemble and glue the two sections which constitute the base of your dish. Take one of the two parts of your second box and glue the bottom on to the base. Paint red.

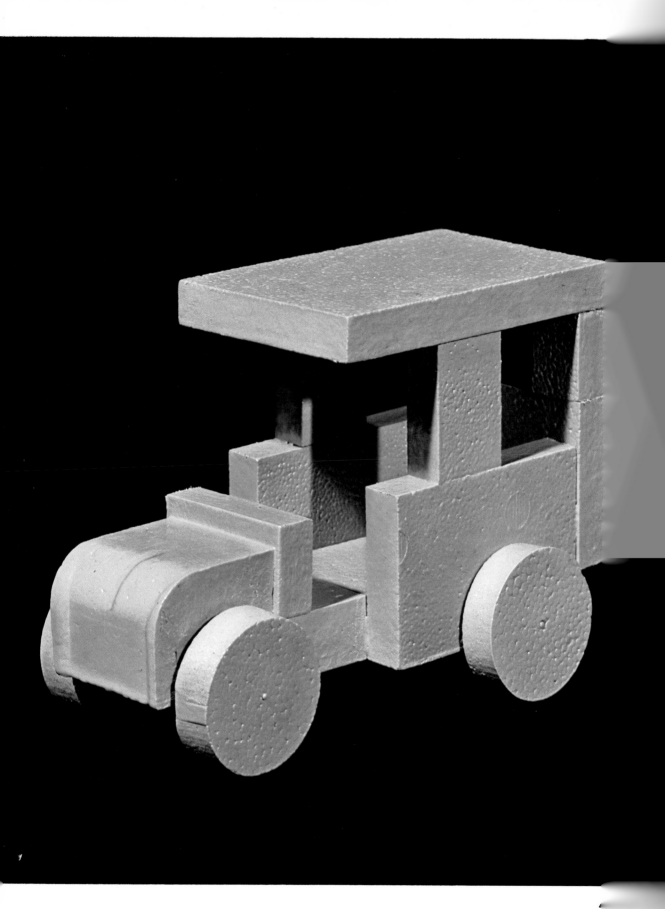

The building game

Materials: slabs of expanded polystyrene (lids of fish boxes, the packaging round boxes of washing powder, etc.); rectangular polystyrene 6-egg boxes; vinyl glue; acrylic paint or gouache.

Here are a few ideas which will help you to create various objects of your choice: sculptures, architectural scale models, etc. From the 6-egg boxes (which consist of two identical parts) cut out the central portion: close the box, lay it flat on a table, then with the help of a cutting-knife and ruler, cut the rectangle to its base; turn the box on its other side and proceed in the same way. With several boxes you will have a series of units capable of being assembled in twos or fours, in a line or staggered (to form a girder support) etc. (on the right in the photo).

If you possess the little hot-wire cutter shown on page 11 (fig. B), you can undertake the following operations:

1) First, cut out of the same thickness of polystyrene a great number of pieces of varying sizes, as shown in figure A. You will then have a great variety of possibilities for building designs. You can glue the components of the construction, paint it, and so keep it.

2) Make a semi-circular arch by cutting the edges of your square or rectangular pieces, at an angle of 60°, then glueing the edges one to another (see photo). To make a pyramid, cut in the same manner the four surfaces of a block, holding the wire at an angle as shown in figure B.

3) To make a cone, angle the wire as shown below, proceeding as for a cylinder (see p. 11).

4) If you don't possess a polystyrene block you can make one by glueing several flatter pieces on top of one another. The cylinder in the photo has been constructed in this way.

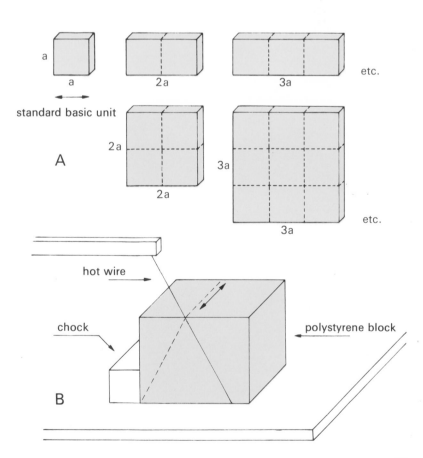

a

a

standard basic unit

2a

etc.

3a

A

2a

2a

3a

3a

etc.

3a

hot wire

chock

polystyrene block

B

47

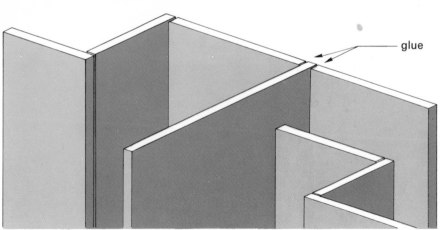

glue

arrangement of panels

Theatrical scale model

Materials: fish-crate lids; insulated ice-cream containers; fine sandpaper; vinyl glue.

This photograph shows an example of the sort of thing you can easily achieve with the help of the simplest materials, without in any way diminishing the interest of your scale model. It's for you to visualise an interesting stage set and bring it to miniature life.

Here are a few details concerning the construction of this scale model: the sketch opposite shows the principle adopted in determining floor plan and space: each panel is glued at right-angles to another. The staircase is made by superimposing $\frac{1}{2}$ in./12 mm. thick pieces one on top of the other. The plinths are made from the ice cream boxes, from each surface of which a thin layer is removed in order to make a neat finish. The relief pattern on the door is achieved by arranging in staggered rows small rectangles of 2 different thicknesses. The picture-frame, top right, is cut from the lid of an ice-cream container. Cut out each piece as indicated on p. 11 and rub all surfaces gently, thus obtaining a clean and velvety-white finish. You can keep them like this or colour with acrylic paint.

treasures
created
from
cardboard
tubes

DUMB-DUMBS

Materials: Cardboard tubes of various sizes; egg-box with round cups; cardboard; strong drawing-paper; tracing-paper; crêpe-paper, pink and black; opaque beads; gilt string; a fancy button; a small safety pin; a ribbon; glue; gouache.

Hand-puppets consist of a head attached to the end of a hand-held stick. This stick is sometimes encased in an outer covering into which the hand is inserted. Those shown here, apart from the two birds, are encased in a cardboard tube for insertion of the hand.

The minister of injustice (left foreground)

Take a tube $6\frac{1}{4}$ in./16 cm. long, with a diameter of $3\frac{5}{8}$ in./9·5 cm. For the shoulders, trace the sketch on p. 55, transfer on to cardboard and cut out. Glue the shoulders on to the tube. For the epaulettes, split in two lengthways a tube $1\frac{1}{8}$ in./ 3 cm. long and $2\frac{1}{4}$ in./55 mm. in diameter, and glue these two pieces under the cardboard of the shoulders. Then take two tubes which can slide, one into the other, one of which will be about $2\frac{1}{4}$ in./ 55 mm. in diameter. From the smaller tube cut a $4\frac{5}{8}$ in./11·5 cm. length (the head). From the larger tube, cut a $1\frac{5}{8}$ in./45 mm. length (the hat) and a $\frac{5}{8}$ in./15 mm. length (the stand-up collar). Glue these together, then glue on to the body; and at the top of the hat glue a circle of cardboard $3\frac{1}{8}$ in./8 cm. in diameter. Cut out of drawing paper the scarf F and G, previously traced, and glue to the edge of the cardboard which forms the shoulders (F in front of G). Paint the puppet as shown.

Soldier on parade

Cut a $16\frac{1}{2}$ in./42 cm. length from a $3\frac{1}{8}$ in./8 cm. diameter tube. Its closed end will make the kepi. For the arms glue to each side of the body a tube $5\frac{7}{8}$ in./15 cm. long and $\frac{3}{8}$ in./ 35 mm. diameter. Cut out of cardboard the kepi's vizor, D, and the epaulettes, C, (traced from the sketch on p. 55). Glue and paint. Glue the gilt strings to the edges of the epaulettes. Make the medal with a small safety pin, a fancy button and a ribbon, then glue on to the tube.

53

A Russian doll

Take a postal tube (3⅛ in./18 cm. in diameter) with a stopper to make the doll's hat. Cut a length of 10 in./25 cm. and paint your doll.

Bird of good omen (second from the right)

Paint black a 10 in./25 cm. long tube, 1⅜ in./3·5 cm. diameter. Cut a fringe 2⅜ in./6 cm. long in a band of pink crêpe paper 12 in./30 cm. long by 3⅛ in./8 cm. wide. Put a band of glue inside the base of the tube. Roll up the crêpe paper, insert into the tube leaving the fringe showing and stick the paper down firmly. The neck is in drawing paper: trace sketch and transfer on to the drawing paper; cut out and fold as indicated; paint it grey, then glue to the end of the tube. For the head, cut out, following sketch A, an egg-box with rounded cups. Glue 2 large opaque glass balls or cork balls to the bottoms of the cups to make the eyes. Slit the beak. Paint the head and comb as in the photo and glue it to the top of the neck.

Bird of ill omen (extreme right)

Cut a 14⅛ in./36 cm. length from a 1⅜ in./3·5 cm diameter tube. A band of black crêpe paper 29½ in./75 cm. long by 3⅛ in./8 cm. wide, fringed to a height of 2⅜ in./6 cm., is rolled obliquely round the tube, beginning at one end and finishing 4¾ in./12 cm. from the other. Hold the tube upright, and roll, beginning at the base, the fringe going over the top of the tube (glue only the two ends of the band). When the tube is turned over, the fringe will fluff out. Cut the two pieces of the beak, H, out of strong drawing paper, glue them together, and paint maize yellow. Glue the beak high up on the tube. Just above the beak, glue two opaque glass balls, previously painted, for the eyes. Paint the tube black.

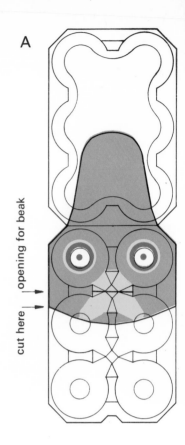

A

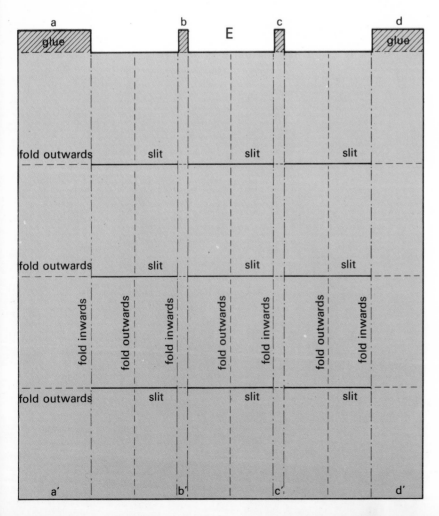

F

the minister's scarf

edge to glue

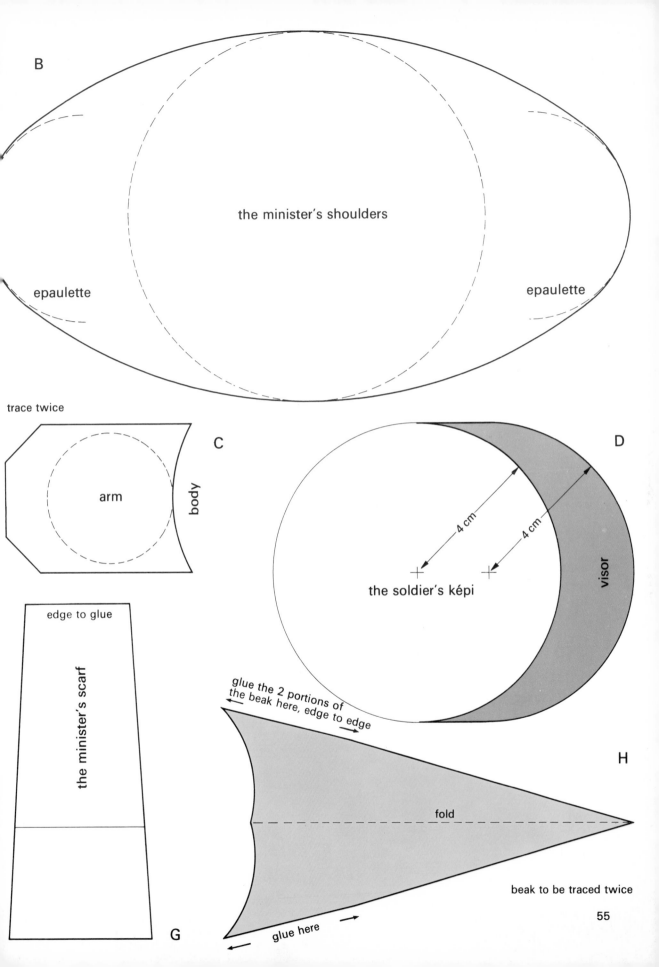

B

the minister's shoulders

epaulette

epaulette

trace twice

C

arm

body

D

the soldier's képi

4 cm

4 cm

visor

edge to glue

the minister's scarf

glue the 2 portions of
the beak here, edge to edge

H

fold

beak to be traced twice

55

G

glue here

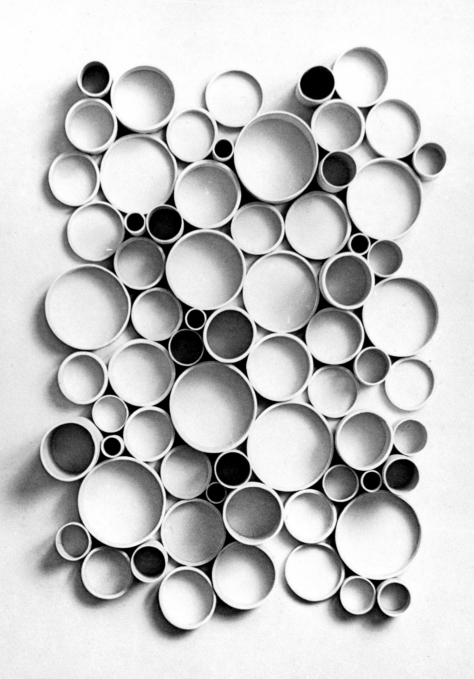

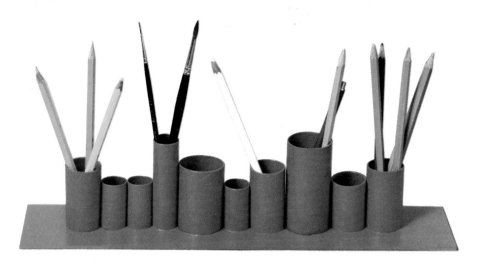

Pencil holder

Materials: rigid cardboard 15¾ in./40 cm. × 3½ in./9 cm.; cardboard tubes of 1 in./24 mm., 1⅜ in./34 mm. and 1⅝ in./42 mm. diameter; glue; coarse sandpaper; red lacquer paint.

From a 1 in./24 mm. diameter tube cut 3 tubes 1¾ in./43 mm. long and one of 3¼ in./83 mm.; from a 1⅜ in./34 mm. diameter tube cut one tube 1¾ in./43 mm. long and 3 of 2⅜ in./60 mm.; from 1⅝ in./42 mm. diameter tubes cut one tube of 2⅜ in./60 mm. and one of 3¼ in./83 mm. Rub the cut edges with sandpaper. Trace a line lengthways along the middle of the cardboard plaque; at 1⅝ in./4 cm. from one end start glueing the tubes next to one another on to the cardboard along this line, in the order shown in the photograph. Lacquer everything red.

Relief picture

Materials: cardboard tubes approximately 1⅜ in./35 mm. and 2 in./50 mm. in diameter; plank of plywood ⅛ in./3 mm. thick; coarse sandpaper; fine sandpaper; white matt acrylic paint; white paint in spray container.

Cut the tubes of different diameters in pieces of varying heights; place them on your cardboard, looking at them from above but also from each side (pay special attention to the shadows). Rub the cut edges with coarse sandpaper. Paint the tubes with acrylic paint and rub the downy bits with fine sandpaper. Having decided on the placement of your tubes, glue them down on to the cardboard, starting at the centre and going round it. Use little glue to avoid leaving traces. Paint with the spray in several short bursts, spraying again when each coat has dried.

Napkin rings

Materials: a tube of strong cardboard 2 in./50 mm. in diameter; coarse sandpaper; lacquer paint—blue, red, black, green and gold.

Cut the tube in rings 1¼ in./33 mm. high, as many times as you require rings. Smooth the cut edges with sandpaper, lacquer the rings blue and allow to dry. Trace the design at the right, transfer on to the napkin rings and, using a very fine paintbrush, fill in the colours of the design.

57

29

34

roof

A

3 · 3

3

B

6

34

27

floor of tower

cat-walk

19

20

5

flagstaff

20

82

C

façade D

50

43

21

D

43

9

45

20

flagstaff

24·5

7

36

30

33

E

14   14

Fort Wood

Materials: cardboard tubes in diameters of $1\frac{1}{4}$ in./30 mm., $1\frac{3}{8}$ in./35 mm. and $1\frac{3}{4}$ in./45 mm.; thin, rigid cardboard; double-surfaced corrugated cardboard; glue; acrylic paint, earth red, dark yellow and black.

For the palisade posts, cut the $1\frac{3}{8}$ in./35 mm tubes as follows: 32 tubes $11\frac{3}{4}$ in./30 cm long, 37 tubes 13 in./33 cm. long. Using the $1\frac{3}{4}$ in./45 mm. tubes, cut 5 lengths of $16\frac{7}{8}$ in./43 cm. for 3 corner-posts and the entrance, and 4 tubes $19\frac{5}{8}$ in./50 cm. long for the watch-tower corner-posts. Cut 4 tubes, $13\frac{3}{8}$ in./34 cm. long ($1\frac{1}{4}$ in./30 mm. diameter) for the cross-beams to support the watch-tower floor and roof. Take $1\frac{1}{4}$ in./30 mm. diameter tubes, and cut off $17\frac{3}{4}$ in./45 cm. for the cross beam over the entrance and $27\frac{5}{8}$ in./70 cm. for the flagstaff (see p. 9).

Using a hand-saw, $9\frac{5}{8}$ in./24·5 cm. from the bottom of the 4 watch-tower posts, make a slit $2\frac{3}{4}$ in./7 cm. deep halfway round the tube. Slit the other palisade posts at the same height, a quarter of the way round the tube on both sides to take a piece of cardboard $1\frac{1}{8}$ in./3 cm. square which will hold the posts together (fig. A).

To assemble the entrance (fig. E) make holes $14\frac{1}{8}$ in./36 cm. from the ground in the 2 gateposts big enough ($1\frac{1}{4}$ in./30 mm.) to take the crossbeam. Make more holes in each of the 4 watch-tower corner-posts $8\frac{1}{4}$ in./21 cm. up for the cross-beams to support the floor, and $16\frac{7}{8}$ in./43 cm. up for the roof supporting beams (figs. D and C).

Doors, roof, floor and cat-walk are made from corrugated cardboard. For the door-hinges, slit right along the top layer of the cardboard $\frac{3}{4}$ in./2 cm. from the edge, fold down and glue to the gate-post.

To support the cat-walk cut out 9 rectangles 2 in./5 cm. × $1\frac{1}{4}$ in./30 mm. and glue inside the palisade $9\frac{1}{2}$ in./24 cm. from the ground. Cut three thicknesses of corrugated cardboard for the base of the flagstaff.

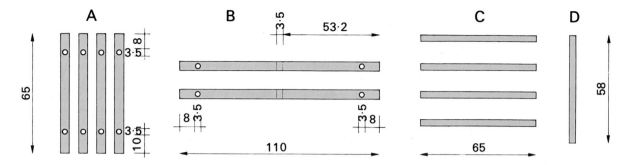

Collapsible table

Materials: cardboard tubes about 1⅜ in./35 mm. and 2 in./50 mm. in diameter; plank of plywood measuring 25⅝ in./65 cm. × 43½ in./110 cm. (to be lacquered red); coarse sandpaper; French chalk, deep yellow acrylic paint.

Cut the table legs: from 2 in./50 mm. tubes, cut four 27⅝ in./70 cm. pieces; at 3⅛ in./8 cm. from one end and 3⅞ in./ 10 cm. from the other pierce each tube right through, cutting out 2 circles 1⅜ in./35 mm. in diameter (see p. 9). Cut the central cross-bars: from 2 in./50 mm. tubes cut two pieces 43½ in./110 cm. long; at 3⅛ in./8 cm. from each end, pierce the tubes right through, cutting out 2 circles, 1⅜ in./35 mm. diameter, and also cut, at right angles to the other holes, two holes of 1⅜ in./35 mm. diameter, in the middle of each tube (fig. B). From the 1⅜ in./35 mm. diameter tubes cut 4 tubes 25⅝ in./65 cm. long and one 22⅞ in./58 cm. long (figs. C and D). Sandpaper the cut edges and, before mounting, give two coats of paint, (the first diluted 1 part paint to 5 parts water). After 24 hours, French chalk the edges of the holes, then through the end holes of the B cross-bars push the C bars, which then pass through the holes in the legs (A); finishing with the centre bar D (22⅞ in./58 cm. long), which unites the two B bars. Rest your table-top on the legs—and when you need more space, simply dismantle.

A heavy-weight stool

Materials: a cardboard maxi-barrel (from your grocer or hardware store) about 11 in./28 cm. diameter; cardboard tubes of all diameters; fine sandpaper; white matt acrylic paint; green lacquer paint; glue; round cushion the same diameter as the barrel (foam plastic with a cloth cover).

Fill the barrel with cardboard tubes of exactly the barrel's inside length until no space is left between the tubes. Remove the metal outer rim of the barrel's lid by cutting the stitching. Place the lid, upside down, on to the barrel. Put the metal rim, covered in glue, between the tubes and the inner surface of the barrel. Apply white acrylic paint and rub down when dry. Lacquer green. Place the cushion inside what was the bottom of the barrel.

A record rack

Materials: a cardboard tube 15¾ in./ 40 cm. long, 2 in./50 mm. diameter; 2 pieces of strong cardboard 2 in./ 50 mm × 3½ in./9 cm.; coarse sandpaper; yellow lacquer paint.

At 2⅜ in./6 cm. from the ends of the tube, and every ¾ in./2 cm. between, cut 15 slits, ⅛ in./3 mm. wide and to a depth of half the circumference of the tube. On the lower surface of the tube at 1⅝ in./4 cm. from each end make a further slit, again to a depth of half the tube's circumference and into these slits introduce the 2 pieces of cardboard. Rub down and lacquer yellow. The slits can be made wide enough for records by holding two handsaws side by side when making each slit. Or use one saw and enlarge the slit by rubbing with coarse sandpaper.

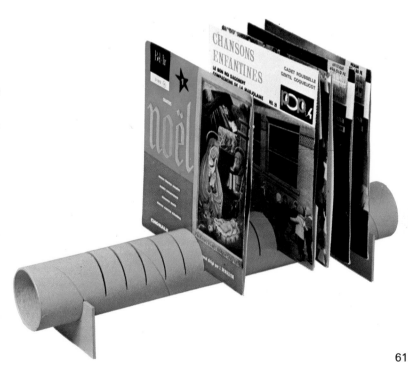

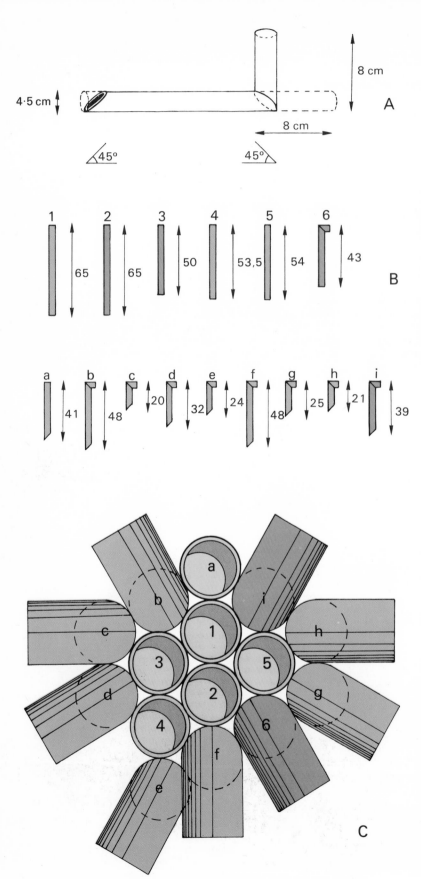

Sculpture—organ pipes

Materials: cardboard tubes about $1\frac{3}{4}$ in./45 mm. diameter; glue, coarse sandpaper; fine sandpaper; white matt acrylic paint; maize, lime, orange lacquer (a spray container is ideal).

Sketch B shows each of the parts which make up this sculpture, with their respective dimensions and colours. You will find it easy to make the diagonal cuts at the ends and at the elbow-bends if you use the 45° slits in the mitre-box (see p. 9). Sketch A shows how to make the elbow-joins; trace a line at the bottom of your box, $3\frac{1}{8}$ in./8 cm. from the slit (in front of you) which will serve to guide your saw; place the edge of each tube on this line and saw. Glue at right angles, to the slit of the longer tube, the $3\frac{1}{8}$/8 cm. portion; proceeding in the same manner for all the elbow-joins. Paint each tube with white acrylic paint, on the outsides and such inside parts as show. Wait for 2 hours, then rub down. Paint the visible interiors of all the tubes maize yellow. If you use a paint-spray, protect the outside of the tube with a piece of rag held round the opening, and spray the interior surfaces with short, sharp bursts. Paint the outsides of the tubes in lime or orange, as shown in sketch B. If using a spray, protect the opening of the tube by placing the opening against a flat surface. To identify each tube mark its back with a letter or a number, following the plan in sketch B. Sketch C shows the placement of each tube, with its reference number or letter (viewed from above). Mark on your tubes the places where they touch one another as a guide for applying glue. Begin glueing at the centre, following first the order of the numbers then of the letters. The heights at which the various tubes should be glued are: tubes 1 to 6 are in contact with the table; a and b are $2\frac{3}{8}$ in./6 cm. above the table; c is at $7\frac{1}{2}$ in./19 cm. above; d at $4\frac{3}{4}$ in./12 cm.; e at $6\frac{1}{4}$ in./16 cm.; f at $2\frac{1}{2}$ in./6.5 cm.; g at $8\frac{3}{4}$ in./22.5 cm.; h at $6\frac{1}{2}$ in./16.5 cm.; and i at $2\frac{3}{8}$ in./6 cm. These figures represent the distance from the base of the tube (or tip of diagonal cut) measured from the table on which sculpture stands.

treasures created
from round
cardboard boxes

The totem pole

Materials: 5 cardboard 'barrels' without handles (one lid); cardboard tubes; double-surfaced corrugated cardboard; thin cardboard; wooden stick; glue; white matt acrylic paint; powdered gouache.

To stick the barrels together, either glue them with a soft vinyl glue; or, for greater solidity, use the method shown in the sketch of the inside of the totem pole. The 5 barrels are attached, either by their bases, or by their open ends. To assemble two bases, pierce a hole in the middle of each base and round this out, using a wood rasp; place in this hole a cardboard tube which is itself pierced through with a small stick of wood. Stop this tube at exactly the level of the next barrel's base by inserting another piece of wood. To assemble two open ends, cover well with glue the outside of a piece of cardboard the right length to go round the inside of one barrel. Insert it to half its height inside the opening of one barrel, then bring the opening of the second barrel down on to the cardboard. The 'wings' near the top of the pole are cut from corrugated cardboard and inserted into slits cut in the pole. For the beak, cut in half lengthways two small tubes of different diameters and glue them one on top of the other. Pierce a hole in the totem pole and insert the beak. For the other protruding features, glue on some cardboard half-tubes. At the top of the totem pole, place upside down, and glue in, a barrel lid from which you have removed the outer rim. Paint the pole with an undercoat of white acrylic paint; after it has dried, paint as the fancy takes you. Put stones or gravel in the bottom of the pole for stability.

Tom-toms

Materials: cardboard barrels without handles or lids; stick of wood; small piece of fabric; string; white matt acrylic paint; gouache in powder form.

Paint the barrels with white acrylic paint; when dry paint the base a bright colour and decorate. Make a fabric ball; pierce and glue it to the end of the wooden stick, and decorate the handle.

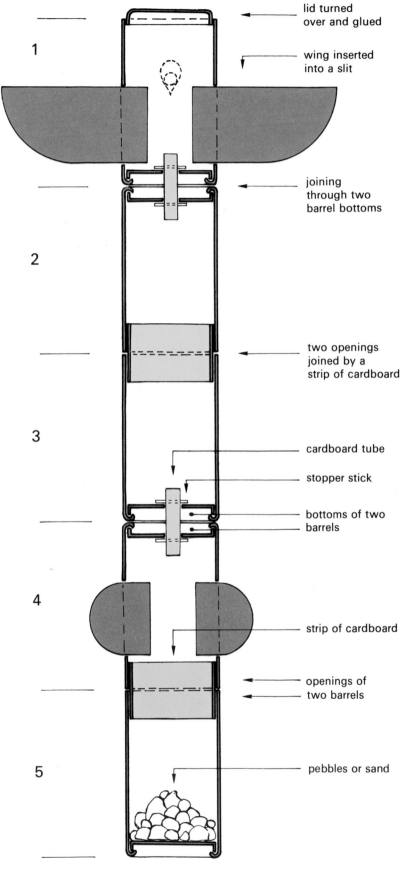

1 — lid turned over and glued

— wing inserted into a slit

— joining through two barrel bottoms

2

— two openings joined by a strip of cardboard

3

— cardboard tube

— stopper stick

— bottoms of two barrels

4 — strip of cardboard

— openings of two barrels

5 — pebbles or sand

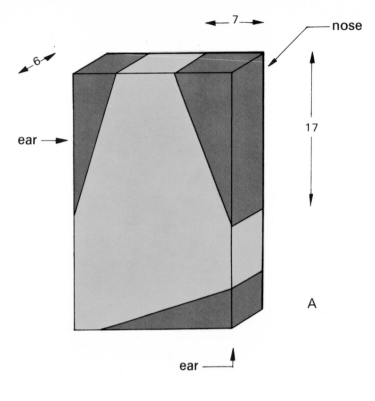

7 →

← 6

nose

ear →

17

A

ear

Little "Carrot-top"

Materials: cardboard container barrel, $7\frac{7}{8}$ in./20 cm. diameter, without handles or lid; large rectangular washing-powder box $2\frac{3}{8}$ in./6 cm. deep; a cardboard tube $2\frac{3}{8}$ in./6 cm. diameter; an egg-box with angular cups (see p. 10); crinkly orange and black fibre paper used in packing fruit; glue; fine sandpaper; white acrylic paint; pale green lacquer paint; gouache.

Turn the barrel upside down. Make an opening $2\frac{3}{8}$ in./6 cm. long and 2 in./5 cm. wide, $3\frac{3}{4}$ in. from the bottom (now top) of the barrel. From the rectangular box cut out nose and ears as shown in sketch A, The slanting end of the nose and of each ear piece is cut out, folded and glued as shown in sketch B. Round out the portions of these 3 pieces where they come into contact with the curved surface of the barrel. Glue the nose into the hole you have just cut in the barrel, and the ears in line with the head, at $5\frac{3}{4}$ in./ 14·5 cm. from the base. At $\frac{3}{4}$ in./ 2 cm. below the base of the nose glue a small piece of tube $1\frac{5}{8}$ in./ 4 cm. long, $2\frac{3}{8}$ in./6 cm. diameter. Cut away the upper half of the circle made by the tube. Then from the egg-box cut out two angled cup bottoms for the eyes, and glue these on. Paint a pale green. Allow to dry, then paint the eyeballs white. To make irises and pupils, paste on each white eyeball a circle of sky-blue paper, $\frac{3}{8}$ in./1 cm. diameter, and in its centre a small black circle. For the hair, make your red crinkly paper into hanks and keep these in place with adhesive bands encircling the top of the barrel making sure the 'hair' covers the top of the 'head'. With a pair of scissors create a hair-style to your taste. Glue on the moustache. Glue on black crinkly paper (or white, painted black) to make the eyebrows. At $5\frac{1}{8}$ in./13 cm. from the base of the barrel, pierce two little holes, one each side of the nose, through which you can look out.

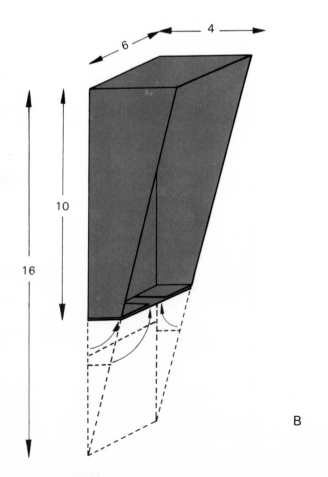

4 →

← 6

10

16

B

Warrior's helmet

Materials: one cardboard container-barrel, $7\frac{7}{8}$ in./20 cm. diameter, without lid; a piece of cardboard; glue; coarse sandpaper; fine sandpaper; tracing paper; white matt acrylic paint; small pots of lacquer paint, metallic green and red.

Shorten the barrel in height by removing a band of $2\frac{3}{4}$ in./7 cm. from the open end. Trace design A on p. 73; transfer it on to your barrel: place the tracing, back to front on the barrel, the base coinciding with the edge of the barrel and go over the traced lines again with your pencil. Cut out (see p. 9). Trace designs B and C (p. 72), then transfer these to a separate piece of cardboard. Make the slits a and a' to the thickness of your cardboard, and glue one on top of the other. Then glue B and C to the top of the helmet. Rub the cut edges with coarse sandpaper. Paint green, then decorate with a red line as shown in the photo.

The witch-doctor

Materials: 2 cardboard barrels $7\frac{7}{8}$ in./20 cm. diameter; a piece of cardboard; coarse sandpaper; fine sandpaper; tracing paper; glue; white acrylic paint; red and black lacquer; green fluorescent paint.

Trace designs D and E, pp. 72 and 73. On to the first barrel trace design D twice (the beak), making sure that the base is in line with the opening of the barrel. Cut out and rub cut edges with coarse sandpaper. Then, just above the cut-out area of the barrel, trace another line, parallel to the base. Transfer design E twice, once with the tracing reversed, to make the 2 ears, placing the base of the tracing on the new line. Cut out and rub down edges with coarse sandpaper. From the other barrel, at 3 in./7·5 cm. from the bottom (barrel turned upside down), make an opening $2\frac{3}{8}$ in./6 cm. high by $3\frac{1}{2}$ in./9 cm. wide, and glue to this opening the two parts of the beak. Glue on the ears, with the pointed ends downwards. Paint the whole head white. Allow to dry, then rub down any small irregularities with fine sandpaper. Lacquer red. To make the eyes, cut out 2 cardboard circles of $2\frac{3}{4}$ in./7 cm. diameter and 2 of $\frac{1}{2}$ in./15 mm. diameter; paint the large circles in fluorescent green and lacquer the small ones black. Glue the small circles on to the middle of the large ones; then glue the eyes on to the barrel at $7\frac{7}{8}$ in./20 cm. from its base and at each side of the middle of the 'face'. Trace and transfer to a piece of cardboard design F (the eyebrows). Cut out, rub down and curve inwards by manipulating several times between thumb and forefinger. Lacquer black, and glue the shaded portion (in the design) between the eyes.

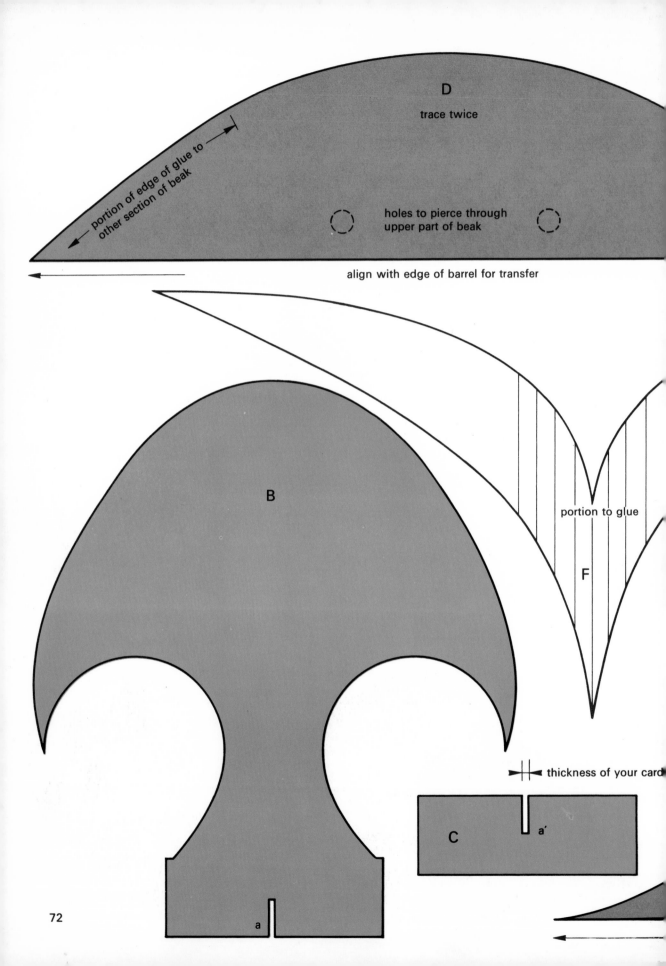

D

trace twice

portion of edge of glue to
other section of beak

holes to pierce through
upper part of beak

align with edge of barrel for transfer

B

portion to glue

F

thickness of your card

C

a′

a

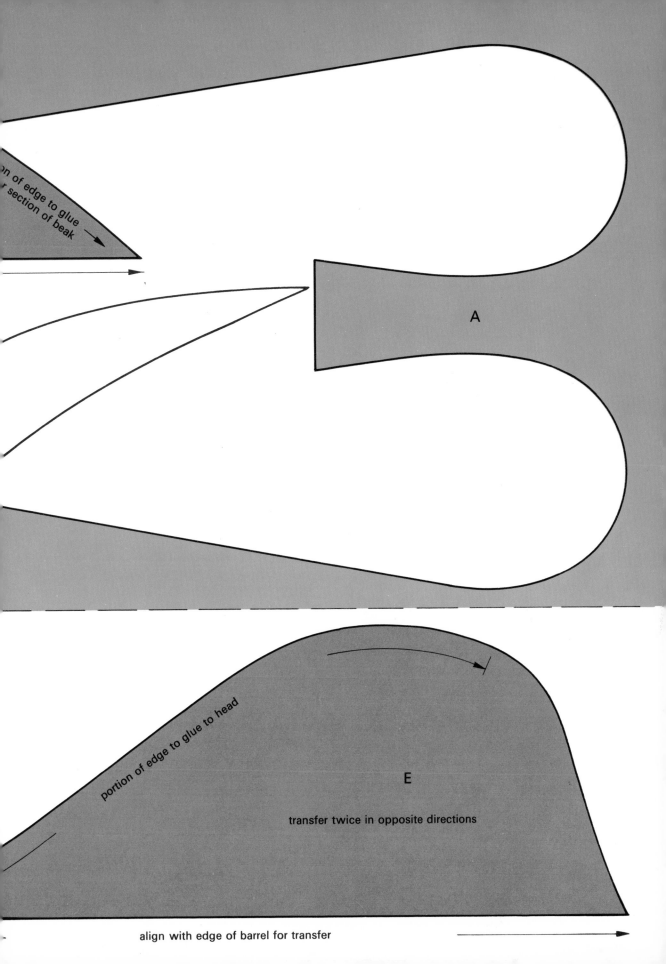

...on of edge to glue
...r section of beak

A

portion of edge to glue to head

E

transfer twice in opposite directions

align with edge of barrel for transfer

treasures created
from
aluminium foil

Metal leaf

Materials: aluminium foil; a poplar (or other) leaf, reduced to its skeleton state (after lying for some time at the foot of a tree); glue (rubber cement or better still a spray adhesive); thin cardboard $5\frac{7}{8}$ in./15 cm. square; thick white cardboard for mounting $11\frac{3}{4}$ in./30 cm. × $9\frac{1}{2}$ in./24 cm., soft thick flannel; a plank of wood; a mallet (or a hammer).

Cover the thin cardboard with a light, even coating of glue. Place your leaf carefully in the middle and make it stick at once by fingertip pressure. Place over everything a sheet of aluminium foil larger than the cardboard, then cover with a thick, flannel-type material; then a plank of wood larger than the aluminium foil. Hold down and, using the mallet, hammer strongly over the entire surface. Gently free your collage, and finish by making the aluminium foil adhere to the spine and veins of the leaf by pressing, not rubbing, with a finger covered with flannel. Then turn your cardboard over on to the flannel, fold back the edges of the aluminium foil on to the back of the cardboard, and glue down. Then carefully glue the whole thing in the centre of a piece of white cardboard, pressing gently with the flannel.

Relief print

With this method, derived from that used to make the metallized leaf, you will be able to take several prints from a composition created with plants from your garden.
To obtain a 'plate', take a thick piece of cardboard (mounting type), or, better, a sheet of plexiglass. Glue your plants to it in the arrangement you have decided upon. Let the glue dry to the stage where no extraneous matter will stick to it. To take a print place on your 'plate' a sheet of aluminium foil covered with a piece of flannel material and press with a small hand-press; or proceed as for the metallized leaf, above. Take up your sheet of aluminium very carefully—it is your first 'print'; you can continue in the same way to make others. It is a good idea to frame each fragile print without delay: cut two pieces of mounting cardboard, larger than the print. In the centre of the first place your print and glue down the top edge; on the second, cut out an opening smaller than the print, so that the edges of the frame cover those of the aluminium foil. Glue the two pieces of cardboard together.

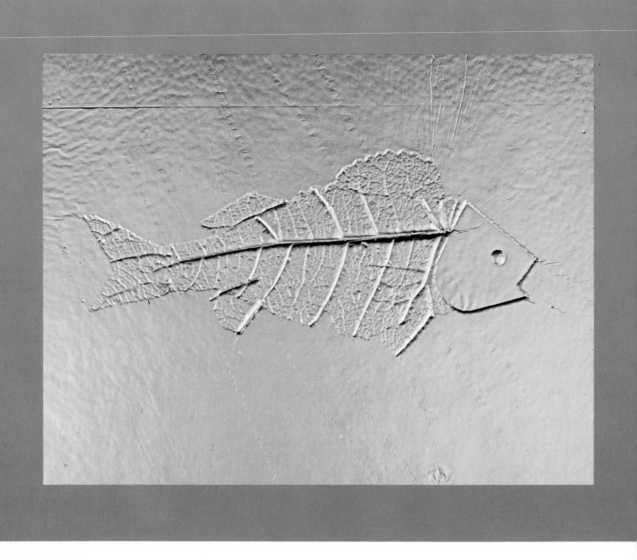

Fossilized fish (an impression in depth)

Materials: A piece of hard cardboard (or plexiglass); dried leaves, with veins showing; a piece of thin cardboard; a plaque of expanded polystyrene; glue; aluminium foil; small press (or plank of wood plus heavy books).

With the help of the above photo, design a fish on heavy cardboard. If you're using plexiglass, first execute your design on a sheet of drawing paper, which you then place over the plexiglass. The skeleton of the fish is made from those of the leaves; cut the leaves with fine scissors, and glue each piece to your design (or to the spine). Allow to dry. Cut the head of the fish out of thin cardboard. Spread a thin coating of glue (vinyl or spray adhesive) on to polystyrene and place on top of this a sheet of aluminium foil. Immediately place your fish skeleton in contact with the aluminium foil, then, carefully, strongly press the whole arrangement. Take out your print and finish by using an aluminium and polystyrene cutter, to obtain a clean edge. During this last operation, protect the fossil with thin cardboard and do not press down too hard on it. You can make a great number of fossil fish by starting again in the same way with fresh pieces of polystyrene and aluminium foil.

Textured heron

Materials: a knitted 'grill' with tight stitches; strong drawing paper; one or several plaques of expanded polystyrene; aluminium foil; vinyl glue or spray adhesive; old biro containing no ink; drawing pins.

On a sheet of paper make the design which you wish to reproduce—one which will consist, as much as possible, of surfaces without details. Trace each item and transfer on to strong drawing paper (inverting your tracing on to the drawing paper and going over the lines with a pencil). Cut out. Place the drawing paper over your grill and glue in their places all the items you have cut out. During this operation keep everything in place with 2 drawing-pins. Allow to dry: your 'plate' is finished. To make prints place a sheet of aluminium foil on the polystyrene plaque (which you have covered with a light coating of glue) and place above your plate (cut out pieces touching the aluminium foil). Hold all together with one hand while with the other tapping the entire surface with a rag made into a ball, or simply with the finger-tips. Remove your grill, and start again in the same way to obtain further prints. With the old, inkless, biro, it is possible to sign each print (not pressing too hard) and to perfect your work by adding details to the untextured surfaces. With this method, you can profit from the advantages of the support (polystyrene and aluminium foil) to make designs in depth directly on to the material with your biro, or even to make imprints of objects in low relief: coins, sand, etc.

endpiece

Puppet theatre

Materials: 4 cardboard tubes $46\frac{1}{2}$ in./118 cm. long, 2 in./5 cm. diameter (A, B, C and D); cardboard tubes, $1\frac{3}{8}$ in./ 3·5 cm. diameter—4 of $22\frac{1}{2}$ in./57 cm. length, (E, F, G, H) 5 of $29\frac{1}{2}$ in./75 cm.; (I, J and scenery-holders), 2 of $25\frac{5}{8}$ in./65 cm. (K and L); double-surfaced corrugated cardboard; a sheet of expanded polystyrene $29\frac{1}{2}$ in./75 cm. × $8\frac{1}{4}$ in./21 cm., 2 hemmed pieces of red velvet, $12\frac{5}{8}$ in./32 cm. × $17\frac{3}{8}$ in./44 cm.; 2 metal rings; string; fine sandpaper; glue; matt acrylic paint: white, black and grey; gold paint.

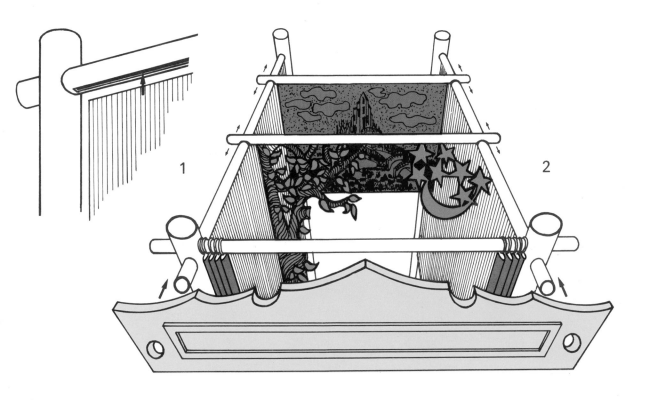

The puppet theatre is entirely dismountable and can accommodate scenery varying with each play enacted, just like a real puppet theatre. It consists of a framework of cardboard tubes assembled at right-angles (see p. 9) and of panels of double-faced corrugated cardboard assembled with the tubes, as shown in fig. 1. The movable scenery is cut out of sheets of corrugated cardboard, fixed into a tube at the top (fig. 6). The curtain is opened and closed from inside, with the aid of string. The animator is seated on the ground behind the theatre. Cut and cut out all the tubes (figs. 3, 4, 5, and 6, p. 84). Only tubes K and L do not pass through the upright tubes. Cut out the panels of corrugated cardboard, orientating them vertically in the direction of their ridges, and insert them into the slits in the horizontal tubes. Assemble these panels with the upright tubes and finish with tube K. For the apron of the stage, fold and glue cardboard over tube L as shown in fig. 8. From a $1\frac{3}{8}$ in./3·5 cm. diameter tube cut 12 rings $\frac{3}{8}$ in./1 cm. wide then sew them to the two parts of the curtain (fig. 9). Pass the rings over tube 1 and attach the 2 metal rings to the upright tubes. Close the curtain and attach the string, with the help of a staple and a drop of glue, to the two central rings. Cut out the pediment (fig. 7) from the sheet of polystyrene, then pierce the 2 holes through which the ends of tubes E and G will pass (fig. 2). For the scenery: cut as many tubes as you will need for background scenery; with a wood-rasp make a rounded notch, $1\frac{3}{8}$ in./3·5 cm. diameter, at $1\frac{5}{8}$ in./4 cm. from the ends of these tubes, then, on the same surface cut a slit into which the corrugated cardboard will fit. For the scenery, cut the cardboard at the top to the maximum width of the stage (fig. 6), pass it obliquely into the theatre until the two supporting bars are reached, then straighten. Paint the tubes white, except for those from which the scenery hangs, which should be painted black. Paint the panels grey on the outside and black inside (indispensable to prevent their buckling). Paint the pediment gold.

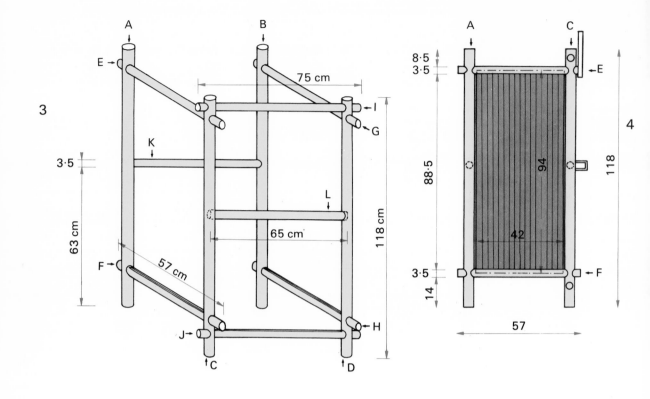

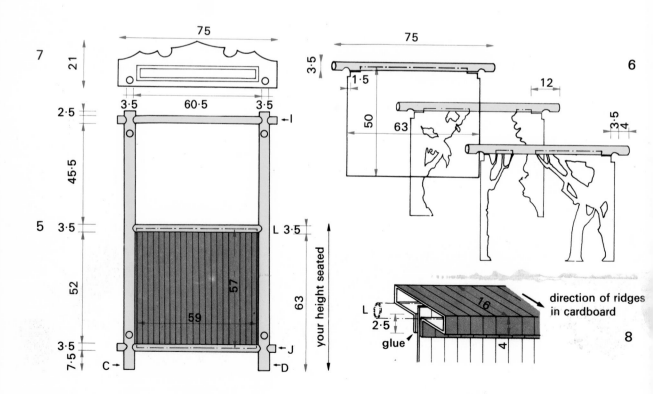

mounting the curtains

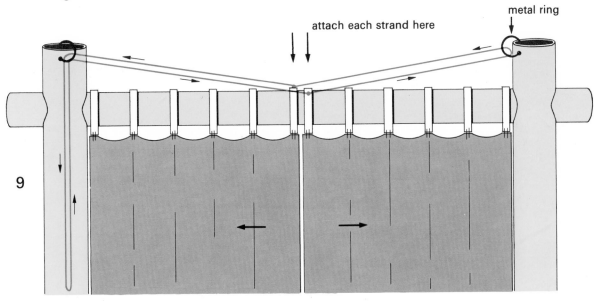

attach each strand here

metal ring

9

helmet for knight (see page **86**)

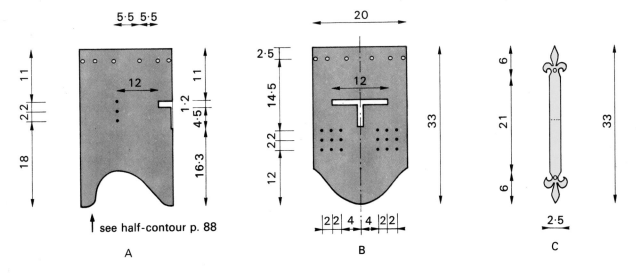

5·5 5·5

11

2·2

18

12

1·2

4·5

11

16·3

see half-contour p. 88

A

20

2·5

14·5

2·2

12

12

2 2 4 4 2 2

33

B

6

21

6

2·5

C

33

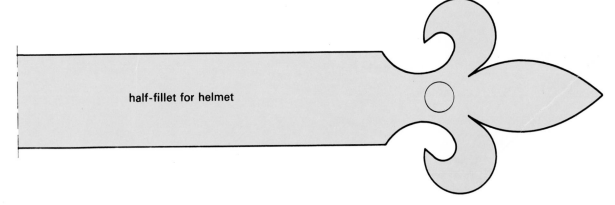

half-fillet for helmet

Knight in armour
Materials: a $7\frac{7}{8}$ in./20 cm. diameter cardboard barrel; two cardboard tubes, $27\frac{5}{8}$ in./70 cm. and $51\frac{1}{8}$ in./130 cm. long, with diameters of approximately $1\frac{1}{8}$ or $1\frac{5}{8}$ in./3 or 4 cm., capable of being fitted one inside the other (tubes from inside rolls of fabric); 8 green nets (used in covering crates of fruit); 5 moulded cardboard platters (for packaging fruit); 2 moulded cardboard 'boats' used in packaging fruit (see sketch of the epaulettes); 2 cardboard kings' crowns; a sheet of ordinary cardboard; bands of gummed Kraft paper; 10 black ribbons $7\frac{1}{8}$ in./18 cm. long; snap fasteners; three large sheets of white crêpe paper; glue; fine sandpaper; little pots of paint: silver, gold and fluorescent orange; white acrylic paint.

The helmet
Remove the bottom of a cardboard barrel without spoiling it, by sliding a paper-knife inside the barrel, and cutting between the bottom of the barrel and the inside lining, going right round the barrel. Turn the cardboard you have removed on to its other surface, and place at the bottom of the barrel. Trace the profile of the border of the helmet (fig. E, p. 88) and transfer on to the base of the barrel. Align the base with the border, go over your tracing, then transfer a second time, continuing the line of the first tracing, having turned the tracing over. Cut out and arrange the openings for the eyes and nose (fig. B, p. 85). At the level of the ears and cheeks pierce holes (figs. A and B), with the end of a cutting-knife with short fixed blade, turning the blade tip from right to left (better still, ask a grown-up to heat up a pointed tool that has a heat-proof handle, and press it gently at each place where you want a hole). Apply an undercoat of white acrylic paint over the whole barrel; leave to dry, rub down any little plushy parts of the cardboard; then apply silver paint all over. After it has dried, attach the top of the helmet with snap fasteners: make a tiny hole for each, through the 2 thicknesses of cardboard, insert the fastener, then bend back the two cardboard edges on each side into the inside of the barrel. For the fillet on the helmet (fig. D, p. 85), cut out, paint with gold and fix in place with snap fasteners down the centre of the helmet, curving it slightly at the nose.

The lance
Cover with glue the end of the smallest-diameter tube, and push it inside the larger. On a sheet of cardboard draw and cut out the spear-head of the lance (fig. F, p. 89) and the lance-guard (fig. G, p. 88). Roll the pieces into their correct shapes and glue them, and hold them in shape with staples. Glue the tip to the end of the lance, and the guard where the two tubes meet (the shorter one serving as the hilt). Paint the lance silver. Between the guard and the tip, roll at an angle a long strip of gummed Kraft paper, which you have previously painted fluorescent: glue down only the two ends.

The coat of mail
Take some trousers and a pull-over, lay them out flat on a newspaper and trace their outlines with pencil. The coat of mail is made from 6 nets folded in two for the trousers and sleeves and 2 nets laid flat for the body. Fold a net in two, lay it on your pattern, cut if necessary on the side of the net edges. Make up, either by sewing or by soldering them together with the aid of a warm iron, placing a piece of tracing paper between the iron and the net and another between the net and the ironing-board. For the body of the coat of mail, lay out two nets flat on to the pattern, cut them, ease the neck-opening, sew the shoulders and the sides (to be worn over dark-coloured tights and pull-over).

The cuirasse
Cut two moulded fruit platters; paint silver. To attach the back to the front attach ribbons: make a slit $\frac{3}{4}$ in./2 cm. from the edge, insert the ribbon and fix with a snap fastener. On a strip of cardboard $1\frac{1}{8}$ in./13 cm. wide glue 2 crowns, side by side, then fix to the cuirasse in a diagonal line, using 2 snap fasteners.

The sleeve of honour
Place 3 pieces of $19\frac{5}{8}$ in./50 cm. $\times$ $12\frac{5}{8}$ in./32 cm. crêpe paper on top of one another, then fold in two lengthways. Draw a scalloped line on the three superimposed edges and cut out the 3 thicknesses together. Paint one surface with orange fluorescent paint, glue them together at the short end, one on top of the other, slightly out of line.

The shield
Cut out moulded cardboard fruit platters; glue the two pieces together by their edges, the rounded side outside. Paint silver. Attach the two circles of ribbon with snap fasteners going through the two thicknesses of cardboard.

The knee-pads
Cut out two sets of 4 rounds from a moulded cardboard fruit platter. Paint silver and fasten around the knees with a snap fastener.

The epaulettes
Paint with silver two moulded cardboard 'boats' for fruit; Fasten them to the shoulders of the cuirasse with snap fasteners.

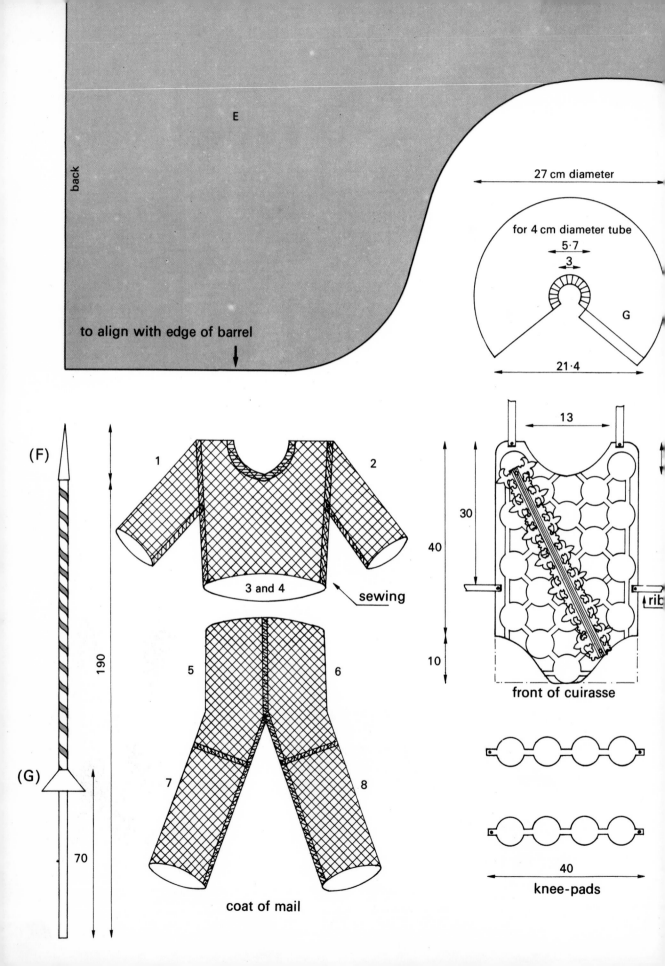

E

back

to align with edge of barrel ↓

27 cm diameter

for 4 cm diameter tube

5·7

3

G

21·4

(F)

(G)

190

70

1   2

3 and 4

sewing

5   6

7   8

coat of mail

13

30

40

10

front of cuirasse

rib

40

knee-pads

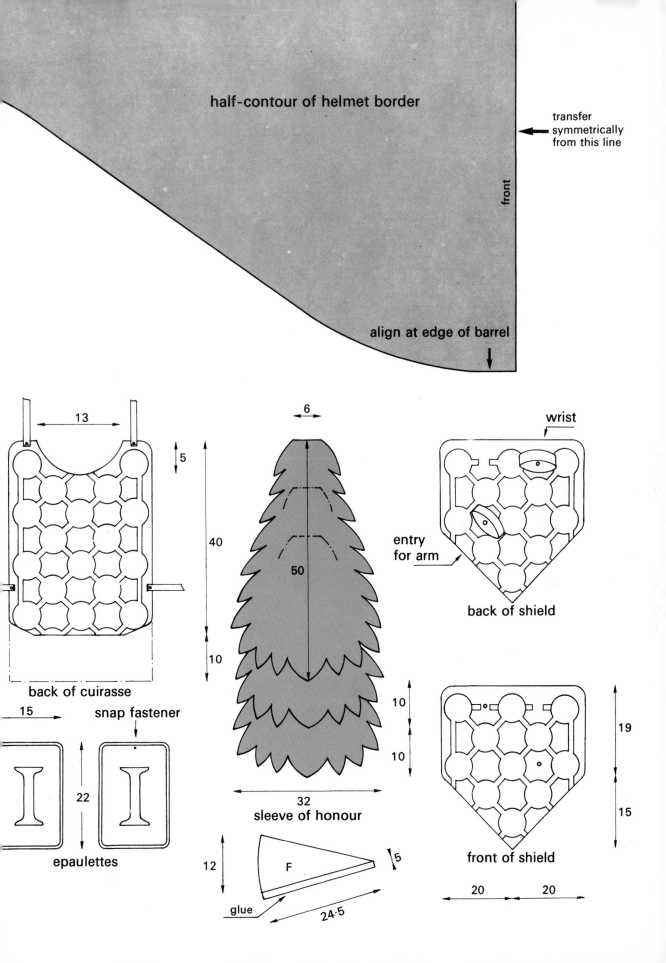

half-contour of helmet border

transfer symmetrically from this line

front

align at edge of barrel

13

5

40

10

back of cuirasse

15

snap fastener

22

epaulettes

6

50

sleeve of honour

32

12

F

5

glue

24·5

wrist

entry for arm

back of shield

10

10

front of shield

19

15

20   20

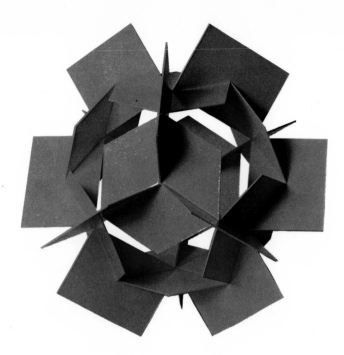

Sculpture I

Materials: pieces of cardboard all the same thickness (for example, those found in boxes of chocolate); tracing paper; carbon paper; spray paint.

For the above sculpture, you will need 8 hexagons and 12 rectangles. Trace carefully the two pieces shown below, using ruler and pencil. Transfer to your cardboard (still using a ruler) with the aid of carbon paper. Cut out all the pieces with great precision and open out each slit: the width of the slits is equal to the thickness of the cardboard. To put your sculpture together, slide the slits of the rectangles into those of the hexagons, at right angles, directing always towards the interior the angle formed by the slits of the rectangles. Paint, preferably with a spray.

Sculpture II

The photo opposite shows a 'sculpture' created by assembling 6 objects similar to Sculpture I. Putting 2 of these together makes a hexagon with 6 slits. The inserted slits receive 3 other rectangles turned in the opposite direction to make a new object. To give more body to the sculpture it is sometimes necessary to place double rectangles between 2 objects: these rectangles measuring $2\frac{3}{4}$ in./7 cm. × 2 in./4·9 cm. with slits at the four angles. For this assemblage you need: 4 hexagons with 6 slits and 36 with 3 slits; 6 double rectangles and 64 single ones.

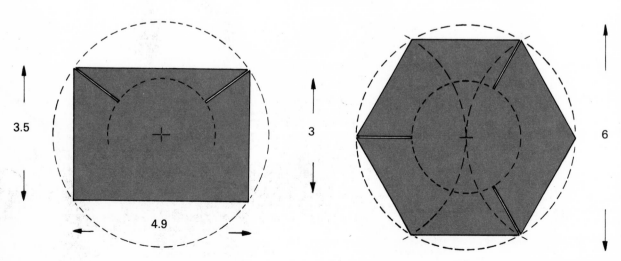

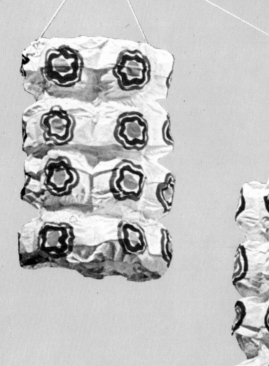

Let's light the lanterns ... the party goes on!

Japanese lanterns

Materials: moulded paper for the packaging of fruit; galvanized iron wire; an office stapler; string; gouache.

Form a cylinder by uniting the two ends of a piece of moulded paper: staple the two edges inside the lantern. Make two circles of galvanized iron wire the same diameter as the lanterns; place a first circle inside the lantern at a distance of $\frac{3}{8}$ in./1 cm. or $\frac{3}{4}$ in./2 cm. from the edge. Fold the edge of the paper back over the wire circle, and staple all the way round. Do the same at the other end of the lantern. Attach to the circle a fine string to hang it up by. Paint the outside surfaces of the moulds with brightly coloured motifs. In this way make several lanterns which you can hang together from a long string.